The Happy Plan

The Happy Plan

The complete diet and lifestyle plan for natural happiness

Charmaine Yabsley

COLLINS & BROWN

For Conn

First published in Great Britain in 2006 by
Collins & Brown
The Chrysalis Building
Bramley Road
London W10 6SP

10 9 8 7 6 5 4 3 2 1

British Library Cataloguing-in-Publication Data:
A catalogue record for this book is available
from the British Library.

ISBN 1 84340 340 4

Commissioning Editor: Victoria Alers-Hankey
Editors: Fiona Screen and Jane Ellis
Design: Jo Knowles

Reproduction by Anorax Imaging Ltd
Printed and bound in Singapore

Contents

Foreword

Whether it's the blues, the Holly Golightly 'mean reds', or a general down-in-the-dumps feeling, we all feel low every now and then. If you're reading this book, it is likely you may have experienced all ranges on the unhappiness scale; after all, you're human. No one has the same emotions all day, every day, and truthfully, would anyone want to? But unhappiness, deep-seated unhappiness, is another story. And that's where *The Happy Plan* comes in. Feeling generally down, or unhappy on a regular basis, is not in itself a reason for serious concern, but left untreated or unaddressed it can lead to genuine depression.

Feeling down is a million miles away from what is experienced by the 340 million people who suffer from medically recognized depression. Genuine depression strikes one in four women and one in ten men during their lifetime and is the most common mental illness around. Simply feeling unhappy, however, affects around nine out of 10 people, and symptoms are varied, ranging from general grumpiness and irritability to more severe, borderline depression.

Broadly speaking, this book is aimed at people who are feeling down and unhappy. The reasons for this may be due to several different factors, but not necessarily any particular incident. For instance, when I first started to write *The Happy Plan*, my boyfriend and I had just moved into our dream house, which we had scrimped and saved for. After six nail-biting months, we were finally given the keys and we plonked our boxes in the living room and opened a bottle of champagne. But then real life hit – I was frantically working on various projects, decorating at night and weekends, plus trying to write this book. Most mornings I woke up with palpitations, a headache, sore throat and would regularly burst into tears for no reason.

Luckily, my partner astutely diagnosed my problem: I was exhausted, I'd just changed contraceptives (see Part 1) and I hadn't been to the gym for almost two months. In short, I was unhappy, but because I hadn't thought about myself or my needs – just which task needed to be completed next – for such a long time, I was an emotional, physical and mental wreck.

I'm not a health guru, fitness trainer or nutritionist, but I do know how it feels when life gets out of balance, and you can't see the wood for the trees. The suggestions in this book are just that – suggestions. I know that it is rather unexciting and boring, but the simple truth is that there is no better way to help you re-find your happy, easy-going self than eating correctly, sleeping soundly, exercising regularly and investing some time in your spiritual growth. Above all, *The Happy Plan* is about rediscovering your sense of adventure and fun.

This book is a prescription that will help you become the content, inspirational and inspired person you want to be. We start by looking at what happiness really is (and what depression is) and learn how to recognize the symptoms of unhappiness. The book is then divided into three parts, designed to work with you as you begin your happiness plan.

Part 1, Happy Hormones, will help you to understand the 'natural' reasons for your mood swings; in other words, your hormones.

Part 2, Happy Food, is all about – yes, food. We all know that we are what we eat. This part will help you to stock your cupboards and fridge with healthy, happiness-giving foods that will not only put the smile back on your face, but give you more energy and motivation too. Once you know how certain foods can affect your moods, you automatically have the means on hand to control them.

Part 3, Happy Life, is all about lifestyle and the activities you can do to really boost your happiness. We look at exercise programmes, relationships, work/life balance, alternative therapies, and hobbies such as gardening or painting that can really tap into your creativity and therefore act as mood-boosters. Enjoy the journey and I hope you not only regain your happiness, but also learn how to hold onto it, even when times get tough.

CHARMAINE

Introduction

The roots of unhappiness

It's important that you recognize the difference between depression and feeling down or unhappy. If you are suffering from genuine depression, you need to seek medical help and start to get to the root of it.

You may be unhappy or feel low because of your circumstances – you've been passed over for that promotion, you've been dumped by your boyfriend, or you just feel grim. It's normal to feel down when you've had an emotional upset. However, if you've had extended periods of feeling blue – when you're not completely depressed, but you are feeling unhappy and don't know why, then it's time to take action. There are several reasons why you might be low and this book will try to help you pinpoint what needs to be changed or adjusted in your life. If you think your mood swings may be connected to your diet, concentrate on the advice in Happy Food, but as happiness is about balance in all areas of your life, I recommend you at least skim the other parts, to help support the areas you need the most work in.

What does happiness mean?

If somebody came up to you and offered to make your most wished-for dream come true, what would it be? Winning the lottery? A trip around the world? The perfect partner? To lose a stone in weight? And how would you feel if you were granted this wish? Undoubtedly, you would answer 'happy'. And there's no denying that you would, at least for a short time. But what about afterwards? What happens once you've spent your million pounds? You may have completed your longed-for trip around the world, but what happens once you've returned home? Your perfect partner may actually turn out to be oh-so boring, and you may realize that losing all that weight didn't magically make life a bed of roses. The truth is, no one is going to stop you in the street and offer to make your dreams come true. The only person who can make you happy is *you*.

Before you start thinking that this is another new-age book, where you learn to 'harness the power within', think again. It is about realizing that happiness is all about achieving balance – the balance between being healthy, feeling fulfilled in your personal and professional life and setting and achieving personal goals. Getting your life in balance is noot always easy. Once you achieve this balance, you'll find the pot of gold at the end of the rainbow – happiness. Balance means treating your body with respect. Whether it's through work, exercise, diet or relaxation, your body is the most important tool you have and your gateway to achieving long-term happiness and contentment. Once you've achieved this balance and happiness, you'll understand that any good that comes your way is a unexpected bonus.

What does depression mean?

Being fed up that you have gone from a size 10 to a size 12, or you had a bad day at work doesn't mean you are depressed. Depression is much more serious: at its most severe, it can mean you find it impossible to get out of bed, to feel excited or happy and that you feel a black cloud is following you around. It is a disorder that affects your thoughts, moods, feelings, behaviour and physical health. People used to think depression was 'all in the mind' and that if you really tried you could 'pull yourself out of it'. Doctors now know that depression is a disorder with a biological or chemical basis, which requires proper treatment. No one is immune from it – depression occurs in people of all social classes and ages, in all countries and all cultural settings.

Sometimes a stressful life event triggers depression. Other times it seems to occur spontaneously, with no identifiable specific cause. Whatever the source, depression is much more than grieving or a bout of 'the blues'. Depression may happen only once in a person's life or it may occur as repeated episodes over a lifetime, with periods that are free of depression in between. For some individuals, it is a chronic condition, requiring ongoing treatment.

In fact, the World Health Organisation predicts that by the year 2020 depression will be the greatest burden of ill-health to people in the developing world, and that by then severe depression will be the second largest cause of death and disability. Depression is also a serious drain on the economy. In 2002 in the United States alone, depression cost an estimated $53 billion in terms of the amount of drugs prescribed and work days lost.

Symptoms of depression

The main symptoms include:

- Feeling sullen
- Feelings of hopelessness, guilt and anxiety
- Loss of interest in things that used to be pleasurable
- Change in appetite
- Change in sleeping patterns
- Inability to concentrate
- A lack of energy or feeling run-down

Causes of depression

Depression can be triggered by a bereavement or other sad event, but when the resulting feelings of sadness and anxiety become out of proportion to the situation and persist longer than what is deemed appropriate.

However, there may be no specific event. The actual causes of depression are still unclear, but one of the most probable explanations is an imbalance of a neurotransmitter (chemical messenger) in the brain called serotonin. A serotonin deficiency, it seems, can cause depression. Serotonin is seen as the brain's mood-elevating and tranquilizing drug, and low levels have been found to have a profound effect on mood and wellbeing. Other factors that can precipitate depression are:
- Familial tendency – those with depression in their family may have a 25 per cent chance of developing the illness themselves
- The loss of a job or social isolation
- Side-effects of certain drugs

- Infections such as AIDS, mononucleosis and viral hepatitis
- Pre-menstrual syndrome
- Rheumatoid arthritis
- Certain types of cancer
- Neurological disorders such as stroke, multiple sclerosis and Parkinson's disease
- Nutritional deficiencies of vitamins B12 or B6

What does serotonin do?

Once a mysterious, scientific-sounding word, serotonin is now bandied about regularly in the media and on food labels. High levels of serotonin boost mood, curb food cravings, increase pain tolerance and help you sleep. Low levels of serotonin can result in depression, insomnia, create food cravings, cause aggressive behaviour, coldness (especially of the extremities) and increase sensitivity to pain.

Serotonin is strongly linked to diet. It is manufactured in the brain from the amino acid tryptophan. The vitamins B6, vitamin B12 and folic acid are also required for serotonin to be manufactured. Smoking or drinking strips the body of these vitamins – and thus serotonin – which is why many people feel down after a big night out.

Treatments for depression

At present, most cases of depression in the Western world are treated by medical doctors, who prescribe a wide range of antidepressant drugs, commonly known as Selective Serotonin Reuptake Inhibitors (or SSRIs) to their patients. The most well-known SSRIs are Prozac and Seroxat. While these drugs can help to alleviate depression, they can also bring a wide range of side-effects. For many people SSRIs are undoubtedly the best prescription for their ailment. However there are a huge number of people currently taking these drugs, who could be treated equally as effectively by non-pharmaceutical methods.

Counselling

It's important to try to get to the source of the depression first, before reaching for antidepressants. In other words, to look at the cause rather than the symptoms. It may well be worth considering counselling and psychotherapy, the so-called 'talking treatments'.

Counselling can be short or long term. It involves talking with someone who is trained to listen with empathy and acceptance. This allows you to express your feelings and find your own solutions.

Psychotherapy

This form of therapy is not usually available on the NHS. It is more frequent and intensive than counselling, and delves more deeply into childhood experience and significant relationships. Most psychotherapists work in private practice. Yet the sad truth is that the majority of people attending GP surgeries for depression are offered antidepressants as the first treatment choice. Don't be afraid to come forward and ask your GP about alternatives.

Your GP may offer you one of the following psychological treatments. The choice will depend on what's available in your area, your own preferences, and how severe your depression is:

Problem-solving therapy Five or six sessions can help people break down their problems into manageable portions and provide strategies for coping with them.

Cognitive behaviour therapy (CBT) This helps to identify and change negative thoughts and feelings affecting behaviour and may last up to 12 months.

Guided self-help This delivers a six- to eight-week therapy programme through self-help books, under the guidance of a healthcare professional.

Interpersonal psychotherapy (IPT) This focuses on relationships. Therapy can continue for up to 12 months.

Painful experiences are hard to talk about, but healthcare professionals understand this. Be as frank as possible, so they can offer you the best help. Don't be afraid to ask questions about your condition. Self-help groups offer the opportunity to meet and share experiences with other

people who are going through the same thing, which can be a great relief. It can break down feelings of isolation and, at the same time, show you how other people cope. Finding that you can support others can help you, too. These groups are often led by people who have overcome depression themselves. Your GP may also put you in touch with a local befriending scheme with trained volunteers who could visit, weekly, to give you practical advice, support and a sympathetic ear.

Antidepressants and opiates

Antidepressants are drugs that relieve the symptoms of depression. They were first developed in the 1950s and have been used regularly since then. There are many types of antidepressants available, but the majority are either 'tricyclic' antidepressants (TCAs), or Selective Serotonin Reuptake Inhibitors (SSRIs). There are also types known as monoamine oxidase inhibitors (MAOIs). The most well-known opiate is morphine. While morphine is extracted from the poppy plant, other opiates, such as fentanyl, are manufactured by pharmaceutical companies either with or without a compound that was initially produced by the flower. Around 20 million people in Britain take some form of tranquilizers each week, and a further 23 per cent of adults take a milder form of mood-boosters.

How do they work?

There are almost 30 different kinds of antidepressant available today, but they all work by altering the way in which neurotransmitters (see page 18) work in the brain. In depression, some of the neurotransmitter systems, particularly those of serotonin and noradrenaline (see page 20), don't seem to be working properly. It is thought that antidepressants increase the activity of these chemicals in our brains.

Opiates work on receptors in the brain and in the nerves to block pain. Doctors use opiates to treat pain after surgery or pain associated with trauma, such as a severe burn. When morphine is overused, a patient may have some sort of physical reaction, which is why doctors prescribe this class of drug judiciously. The use of opiates over time can lead to tolerance, the need for a higher dose, or physical dependence on the drug, but doctors say such conditions are not the same as addiction.

What are antidepressant used for?

Antidepressants are used to treat moderate to severe depressive illnesses. They are also used to help the symptoms of severe anxiety, panic attacks and obsessional problems. They may also be used to help people suffering from problems such as chronic pain, eating disorders and post-traumatic stress disorder.

How well do they work?

Studies have found that after three months of taking antidepressants between 50 per cent and 65 per cent of people will be much improved. This compares with 25–30 per cent of those given an inactive 'dummy' pill, or placebo. It may seem surprising that so many people given placebo tablets experience an improvement in symptoms, but this happens with all tablets that affect how we feel – painkillers for example. Antidepressants do seem to be helpful but, like many other medicines, some of the benefit is due to the placebo effect.

While antidepressants can be an extremely effective form of treatment, ideally they really should only be prescribed by a GP after attempts at treating depression and low moods through more natural means, including counselling, have failed.

Side-effects of antidepressants

As with all drugs, some people react badly to antidepressants, while side-effects can seem quite mild in others. The irony here of course is that these side-effects can be very depressing in themselves.

The overwhelming popularity of SSRIs has been in part due to their apparent 'safety' over more toxic drugs when used improperly. However, there is also an established direct link between the use of SSRIs and suicide and violent behaviour. The reason there are so many side-effects with antidepressants is really due to the lack of full understanding about how antidepressants, and depression, affect the brain. These can vary greatly from case to case. General side-effects of medication are:

- Dry mouth
- Urinary retention and/or gastrointestinal disturbance/diarrhoea
- Blurred vision
- Sedation (can interfere with driving or operating machinery)
- Sleep disruption
- Weight gain
- Headache
- Nausea
- Abdominal pain
- Inability to achieve an erection
- Inability to achieve an orgasm (men and women)
- Loss of libido
- Agitation and/or anxiety

Side-effects of TCAs (tricyclic antidepressants)
Fairly common side-effects of tricyclic antidepressants include dry mouth, blurred vision, drowsiness, dizziness and tremors, sexual problems, skin rashes, and weight gain or loss.

Side-effects of MAOIs (monoamine oxidase inhibitors)
Rare side effects of MAOIs such as phenelzine (brand name: Nardil) and tranylcypromine (brand name: Parnate) include liver inflammation, heart attacks, strokes and seizures. People taking MAOIs may have to be careful about eating certain smoked, fermented, or pickled foods, drinking certain beverages, or taking some medications in combination with the antidepressant, as they can cause severe high blood pressure. A range of other, less serious, side-effects can occur, similar to those experienced with TCAs.

How happiness works

Whether you are happy, angry, sad, tired, hungry or full, it is your brain that makes you aware of these emotions. There's a lot going on up in that cauliflower-shaped organ! Different parts of the brain perform a number of tasks:

● Controls body temperature, blood pressure, heart rate and breathing
● Transmits information about the world through the eyes, ears and nose
● Controls voluntary movement, enabling us to walk, talk, stand or sit
● Controls memory, reasoning and intelligence
● Provides the centre for drives and emotions such as thirst, hunger, pain and pleasure.

Understanding the brain
In order to understand how our moods work, we must first understand the brain. Here's a summary:

1. The brain is made up of approximately 100-billion nerve cells, called neurones. Neurons don't actually touch each other and the gaps between them are called synapses.
2. Neurones gather and transmit electrochemical signals – just like the wires on a computer.
3. Neurons have four basic parts:
    a) cell body (the centre of the neurone)
    b) dendrites – small, branch-like projections of the cell that transmit nerve impulses to the other cells
    c) axon – a long nerve fibre, which carries the electrochemical message away from the cell body down to the end feet or terminals
    d) end feet or axon terminals – the end of the axon, where nerve impulses are passed onto the dendrites of the next neurone.

Every time your brain sends a message to your body, such as 'I'm happy' the following activity takes place:

1. The brain sends the message along the nerve cell.
2. The nerve cell must find a way to jump the gap or synapse, to pass on the message to the other nerve cells. Nerve chemicals, called neurotransmitters, are stored in tiny sacs at the end of the axon terminals.
3. The brain's message travels down the axon and causes some of the sacs to release neurotransmitters.
4. These nerve chemicals jump across the synapse, tickle the next nerve cell to keep the message moving from one nerve to another – just like a baton in a relay race.
5. Once the neurotransmitter has relayed it message, it is broken down or reabsorbed back into the receiving nerve cell's storage space to be sent again.

The role of neurotransmitters?

Your brain contains around 70 neurotransmitters that regulate nerve function, including memory, appetite, mental function, mood, movement and sleep. If just one of these transmitters is disrupted, the follow-on effect to the rest of the transmitters can be dramatic. Many neurotransmitters are composed of either amino acids – protein obtained from your diet – or a fat-like substance called choline (see below), which is also obtained from food. Certain vitamins and minerals, such as the B vitamins, vitamin C, vitamin E, iron, selenium and magnesium, all also needed to manufacture neurotransmitters. If your diet does not have a sufficient amount of these 'helpers', you'll feel grumpy or unable to think clearly. Some neuro-transmitters become more active, or sluggish, depending on what you eat. Over-consuming or dramatically restricting a particular food, such as fats or carbohydrates, can trigger imbalances in neurotransmitters, which may contribute to depression, irritability, food cravings and extreme mood swings.

There are five neurotransmitters whose origins are directly linked to the amino acids in the food we eat.

1. **Tryptophan** Found in meat and milk. This is the building block for serotonin, the feel-good chemical.
2 and 3. **Dopamine and Norepinephrine** Both are influenced by the amount of tyrosine you eat (found in turkey, chicken).
4. **Noradrenaline** This eases depression, curbs hunger and improves memory and mental alertness. It is found in turkey and chicken.
5. **Choline (acetylcholine)** This is the primary chemical carrier of thought and memory. Unlike other key neurotransmitters, acetylcholine is not made from amino acids. Its primary building block is choline, which doesn't have to compete for entry into your brain like the other neurotransmitters. You can improve choline levels by eating foods such as wheatgerm, eggs, taking lecithin, or nicotinaminde (a form of niacin). It is found in beef and other meats, egg yolk, dairy products, wholegrain products, oats, soya foods and nuts.

There are three main groups of neurotransmitters: monoamies, neuropeptides and single amino acids. Of the three groups, amino acids are present in the brain in the greatest quantity. The neuropeptides are made up of two or more amino acids and the monoamines include serotonin, the most important neurotransmitter in terms of happiness.

Terminology checklist

Some of the medical terms used in this chapter may be new to you. Here's a quick reminder:

Monoamines: calming
Dopamine and norepinephrine

These are manufactured from the amino acid tyrosine with the help of folic acid, magnesium and vitamin B12. When your dopamine and norepinephrine levels drop, you're likely to feel depressed, irritable and moody.

Serotonin and dopamine

Your mood and happiness depend on having enough of these two neurotransmitters. When these levels are low, your mood will reflect this, so you'll be unable to cope with stress. If you stress levels raise, adrenalin and cortisol production (see below) is increased to help you deal with levels of stress. However, if the levels of cortisol are inconsistent, this appears to affect how much serotonin and dopamine is actually produced – leaving you with less of these mood-boosters. Your body also becomes less sensitive to these neurotransmitters, so you will actually need greater amounts than normal for a mood uplift.

Cortisol

Cortisol is a steroid hormone released by the adrenal glands (on top of the kdneys). Cortisol is released on a daily basis: in the morning it's higher, in order to make us more alert. At night it's lower, to help us wind down and sleep. Stress causes the levels of cortisol to be disrupted, which in turn affects sleep patterns and energy levels. When your levels of cortisol are disrupted you may feel down and depressed. Part of a vicious circle – if you're feeling unhappy, you're less likely to be able to deal with stress.

Adrenalin

Adrenalin is another of the hormones produced by the adrenal glands. In times of danger, adrenalin plays a crucial role in our primitive 'fight-flight response' – it helps blood (carrying oxygen and sugar) to be pumped around the body faster to feed the brain (to help you make snap decisions) or the muscles (to help you physically react). If you are constantly under stress your adrenal glands can become burnt out, and are no longer efficiently performing their job. If this occurs, you may experience insomnia, anxiety, panic attacks, periods of indecision and depression, and lethargy. Long periods of constant stress can mean that you are permanently tense and your muscles constantly taut and tightly coiled, ready to react.

Neuropeptides: help the body manage pain
Neuropeptide Y (NPY)

NPY is responsible for cravings for carbohydrate-rich foods. As NPY levels increase, so do cravings for sweets. If you've started dieting, your NPY levels start soaring, which is why you'll suddenly want everything in the cake shop! When you wake up your brain receives a message to release NPY. This is why we're tempted to eat pancakes, toast or sugary cereals in the morning. Stress also triggers NPY production, making us reach for a chocolate biscuit, instead of an apple, during a stressful day.

Endorphins

Endorphins are the body's natural means of coping with pain – the body's natural morphine. They help boost pain tolerance, calmness and produce feelings of euphoria and satisfaction. They are released during exercise, laughter, soothing music, meditation, sex and other enjoyable activities. Serotonin and norepinephrine are endorphins.

Amino Acids: vital for health and normal bodily function
Galanin

Galanin influences whether or not you desire fatty foods. When you haven't eaten for a few hours, fatty acids are released into the bloodstream. They travel to the brain and trigger the release of galanin. The high galanin levels then trigger cravings for fat-containing foods. Reproductive hormones such as oestrogen, stress hormones such as cortisol, elevated insulin levels and endorphins also encourage galanin production. This may explain why women who suffer from PMT crave fatty foods.

Quiz – how happy are you?

Are you the neighbourhood grump, or is your natural personality more sparkling than a bottle of bubbly? The three types illustrated here may be exaggerated, but there are elements of them in most of us. Learning more about your personality can help you to achieve the right balance in life.

1. You're late for work and everything is going wrong. You spill tea over your skirt and can't find your purse. Do you:

a) Burst into tears and seriously consider calling in sick to work?

b) Run around searching for your purse, yelling as you go?

c) Take a deep breath, eat an apple, and calmly look for your purse?

2. When you watch a soppy movie with a sad ending, do you:

a) Cry for days and feel as though you've lost a friend or family member?

b) Smile through your tears – it was a good movie?

c) Turn it off halfway through? What a pile of sentimental junk!

3. You promised to babysit for a friend, but another friend calls and invites you to a spa opening with a free massage and manicure, on ther same night. Do you:

a) Call your friend the day before to cancel, with the excuse of being ill, then go to the spa, but don't enjoy it because you feel so guilty?

b) Find a replacement to babysit for your friend and go to the spa opening, even though you are really tired?

c) Cancel babysitting at the last minute, leaving your friend in the lurch, and attend the spa, without a pang of guilt?

4. Your favourite foods are:

a) Sticky toffee pudding, chocolate ice-cream and apple pie?

b) Home-made meals, such as roast dinners and healthy, balanced meals?

c) You prefer to eat out, and have others wait on you?

5. When you go to the gym do you:

a) Prefer to go to an easy class, such as beginners' aerobics?

b) Like to change your routine and alternate between forms of exercise?

c) Train with a personal trainer? It's the only way you'll reach your goal.

Results

Mostly As: The weeping weakling

You say 'yes' to everybody. Wanting to please everybody all the time usually means that you end up pleasing nobody any of the time, and running yourself ragged. Say 'no' the next time somebody asks you to do something that doesn't really fit into your day's plan. You're sensitive, so you know how to say no without insulting others. Just say, 'I'm sorry, but I won't be able to fit that into my schedule today'. Practise and with time you will have more self-esteem and feel that you have a more honest relationship with others.

Mostly Bs: The see-saw

Sometimes you're on top of the world, other times you're lying in the gutter, despairing over your life. Everything that happens in your life is blown out of proportion: you are the star of your very own drama. You like to live life to the full, but overburden yourself with demands. You may go out every night for a week, then stay in, feeling down, the following week. Sometimes we keep ourselves busy because we're afraid of being alone. Making time out to genuinely enjoy your own company will help you feel more grounded and enhance the caring side of your personality, which may be have been hidden by the flurry of activities.

Mostly Cs: The extremist

Wow – you barely have time to sleep! You are so determined not to miss out on anything, you are in danger of burning yourself out. Ask yourself what makes you happy and find out just how much of your day you spend doing what you truly love. There's nothing wrong with running around in the latest styles, as long as you realize that designer clothes truly do not maketh the man (or woman). It is what's inside that really counts. So spend time contemplating your navel: sign up for meditation classes, enjoy a night in watching corny movies (after all, no one will see you laugh or cry), and make a fool of yourself every now and then. You will like yourself much better for it and so will other people.

Part 1
Happy Hormones

Happy Hormones

We all have hormones in our bodies. They help to carry chemical messages from one tissue or organ to another and are responsible for the reproductive system, growth, puberty, and ultimately the management of our overall health and moods.

What are hormones?

Oestrogen and progesterone are the two major female sex hormones and are controlled by the pituitary gland in the brain. During the reproductive years, ovaries produce oestrogen and progesterone, which are releasesed directly into the bloodstream. If too much of a hormone is produced, it is known as hypersecretion; too little is known as hyposecretion.

The female sex hormone, follicle stimulating hormone (FSH) travels to the ovaries, stimulating the follicles (containing the eggs) in the ovaries to mature and to produce oestrogen. It is also responsible for ovulation.

At the time of ovulation, a luteinising hormone (LH) is secreted, also by the pituitary gland, when oestrogen reaches a certain level. The most advanced follicle of one of the ovaries releases an egg that enters the fallopian tube and is available for fertilization.

Luteinising hormone also stimulates the ruptured follicle to grow into a temporary structure called *corpus luteum*, which produces progesterone and prepares the endometrium (lining of the womb) every month for a possible pregnancy. If the egg is not fertilized, hormone production declines. The *corpus luteum* begins to break down and when progesterone drops below a certain level, the endometrium also breaks down and sheds the unfertilized egg over a few days – this is called menstruation.

As oestrogen and progesterone levels drop, the production of FSH is set into motion again, thereby setting the whole cycle to repeat. When women grow older, the eggs in their ovaries diminish, there are fewer follicles available and hormone levels begin to fluctuate. When this happens, it is usually indicates the start of the menopause.

Oestrogen

This is the female sex hormone produced by the ovaries, which are responsible for the development of female sex characteristics and is largely responsible for stimulating the uterine lining to thicken during the first half of the menstrual cycle in preparation for ovulation and possible pregnancy. It is also important for healthy bones and overall health.

Oestrogen and your period: Oestrogen controls the first half of your menstrual cycle, until your eggs leave your ovaries (see Table, pages 28–29).

Oestrogen and your mood: Oestrogen is a stimulant of the nervous system. Too low a level, may result in feelings of depression and lethargy. If your levels are too high, you may experience anxiety, irritability and nervous tension. Ideally, a woman's oestrogen levels should provide a feeling of motivation and stability.

Progesterone

Progesterone performs a range of different functions. It helps to build bones and protects against osteoporosis, helps burn fat for energy, maintains the uterine lining, acts as a natural diuretic, maintains healthy thyroid function, normalizes blood clotting, restores and maintains sex drive and helps prevent breast and endometrial cancer. Most modern steroid hormones have properties based on those of progesterone.

Progesterone and your period: Progesterone is made in the ovaries of menstruating women. It is produced at the time of ovulation and by the placenta during pregnancy.

Progesterone and your mood: If you suffer from low moods around the time of your period, it may be that your progesterone levels are low.

If you feel happier and more energetic when your period starts, or just after it, it indicates that you have high levels of oestrogen. Oestrogen levels vary between women and tend to be lower after childbirth and around and after the menopause. A lack of oestrogen in the body can cause depression. It's believed that oestrogen may help ward off depression during these times by increasing the amount of the feel-good chemical, serotonin, in the brain.

Your monthly cycle

Day	Mood	Recommendations
1–2	This is the first day of your period. You have very little progesterone in your body. Usually you feel energetic, euphoric and positive. You also have very little oestrogen.	If you're suffering from stress and mood swings, take some time out. Be careful driving – you may be clumsier than usual. Avoid sports that require skill and precision as these could leave you feeling frustrated. Concentrate on short, high-intensity workouts or calm yourself down with a yoga or Pilates class. If you suffer from cramps, ditch the hot water bottle and aspirin and opt for a brisk walk or lengths in the pool. Evidence suggests that women who exercise regularly suffer less pain and have shorter cycles. Don't be tempted to push yourself too hard or for too long, though, as your immune system will be susceptible to illness during these days.
3–7	You should feel a little better as your body completes menstruation.	As with days one and two, take it easy physically – get some early nights instead of burning the candle at both ends. Eat around 500 calories extra each day – you need it! Concentrate on foods rich in Omega 3, such as oily fish and nuts, and drink lots of filtered water.

8–13	Oestrogen levels peak just before ovulation (around day 14). You may suffer from bloating – both oestrogen and progesterone are to blame for water retention.	Your body is able to deal with longer workouts. Do fat-burning sessions of running, swimming or cycling. Try a more advanced aerobic, dance or circuit class now, as your body is up for tougher, longer periods of exercise.
14–17	These may be your cranky days! Ovulation is occurring and oestrogen levels are high. Once the egg has left the ovary, the follicle begins producing progesterone. You may feel teary, irritable or depressed for no reason.	Work out your aggression, whether you prefer gentle stretches to ease bloating, or a boxercise or martial arts class that helps you get rid of pent up anger. Acupuncture or massage may also help your system.
18–25	Oestrogen and progesterone levels continue to rise. Mood-wise, you may be feeling tired, cranky and bloated. Some women get pimples around their chin during this time.	If you suffer from tender breasts, wear a supportive bra and choose the right exercise for your symptoms. Increase aerobic sessions on days 20–24, while the body is optimizing fuel supplies – don't overdo it! Aim for three one hour aerobic classes this week.
26–28	If you haven't conceived, progesterone and oestrogen levels begin to fall. Some women experience diarrhoea or constipation, or feel that a fog has lifted and they can think more rationally. You are returning to a similar physiological state as in the early stage of your cycle, so you may feel stressed and emotional. If you suffer from cold sore break-outs, now may be the time to be extra vigilant and apply a medicated lip balm.	Reduce the length, frequency and difficulty of your workouts in days 26–28 in response to your depressed immune system. Stock up on immune-boosting foods and take vitamin C, magnesium and zinc to help ease symptoms.

In the second half of your cycle, you have less oestrogen and more progesterone in your body. The oestrogen receptors in the brain are blocked, which leads to moodiness and a general feeling of flatness, because body and mind aren't receiving as much oestrogen.

Hormones and PMT

Around 80 per cent of women suffer from some form of premenstrual tension (PMT), such as irritability, bloating, food cravings or irrational mood swings. Almost 30 per cent of women are affected further: unable to face friends or family, a constant feeling of helplessness and sadness, bursting into tears at the drop of a hat. Many women are prepared to put up with PMT because they believe that nothing can be done to solve the problem.

Hormones and the pill

An incorrect pill prescription can cause weight gain, acne, lack of libido, mood swings, poor hair condition and, in severe cases, depression. But the correct pill can actually make life (and PMT) much easier. Women and their doctors need to be educated on how to decide which pill should be taken

Different pills contain different levels of the hormones progesterone and oestrogen; problems can arise if you are sensitive to one or other of them. Progesterone is a naturally occurring hormone, which cannot be replicated in the pill, due to its short lifespan. Therefore, a synthetic type, known as progestergen, is used in the pill. A study by the Centre for Mental Health Research in Australia reports that this synthetic hormone can actually cause depression in some women. Progestergen is absorbed directly into the liver, which releases sex-hormone binding globulins. Sex hormones called androgens (produced by the adrenal glands) help to control the libido. Too many androgens in your blood, may result in spots, greasy hair, weight gain and feeling flat and moody. Women who tend to feel this way tend to be progestergen-sensitive and should opt for an oestrogen pill.

How to choose the right pill for you

Combination pill

If you're under 35, don't smoke and have mid- to mild PMT, then an oestrogen pill, such as the combination pill, is ideal. (The combination pill contains mainly oestrogen, with a small amount of progestergen – hence the name combination.) Ask your doctor about the benefits of the following:

Brevinor
Cilest
Conova 30
Eugynon 30
Femodene
Femodette
Loestrin 20
Loestrin 30
Marvelon
Mercilon
Microgynon 30
Minulet
Norimin
Norinyl-1
Ovran
Ovran 30
Ovranette
Ovysmen

Progestergen-only pill (POP)

This contains a progestergen hormone similar to the natural progesterone that women produce in their ovaries. It contains no oestrogen. There are different types of POP available, some containing different progestergens. The progesterone-only pill is best for women with heavy, painful periods, endometriosis or who suffer from migraines prior to their period.

Oestrogen-only pill

Jasmine, introduced to the UK around three years ago, is the only oestrogen pill available. The oestrogen-only pill is best for women who have found that their skin and weight have suffered after taking other pills. It is also ideal for women who become extremely lethargic just before their period starts.

Preventing PMT

When you are ovulating, your body tends to need a little more of everything. It needs more water, more vitamins B6 and B12, iron, calcium, more sleep, more (gentle) exercise and more food. Unfortunately, if you're not paying attention to your menstrual cycle, you won't be prepared for these extra demands, which is when your PMT may spiral out of control.

There are hundreds of ways to treat PMT, but it does come down to your individual preferences and needs. I always make a note in my diary to book an acupuncture appointment exactly one week before my period is due. I also make sure I increase my intake of starflower or evening primrose oil, and I try to resist cravings for wheat during this time. And I do at least 30 minutes of exercise every day for the preceding seven days. After many years of trying different remedies and treatments, I have found that this is what works for me.

Recently, a new phenomenon, called 'post-premenstrual tension' has been identified. As if we didn't suffer enough before our periods, we are now being afflicted all through the month! Breasts are sore and you are irritable for a few days after your period, as well as before. Post-PMT can occur if your body is particularly low in B vitamins, or if you have an especially heavy period.

While the pill can and does prevent the major effects of PMT, taking the pill itself can still cause nutritional shortages in your body, which can make you feel just as bad.

The pill strips the mood-regulator vitamin B6 from your body, and a deficiency can cause moodiness, lethargy or anaemia. It's important to ensure you eat enough B6-rich foods whilst on the pill. Load up on foods such as spinach, peppers, tuna, bananas, liver, turkey breast, snapper and cod just before and during your period. According to the National Association for Premenstrual Syndrome (NAPS), taking around 1.6mg of vitamin B6 a day is recommended for women. Women who suffer from breast tenderness may find taking around 3,000–6,000mg of evening primrose oil a day can help.

Your anti-PMT plan

- Keep a diary of your cycle so you know when your period is due. If you find that acupuncture, or some other form of alternative remedy, helps, schedule this in, as you would a doctor's or dentist's appointment.
- Take a supplement specially formulated to balance hormones (see Further Information for recommended stockists).
- Write a daily reminder that you could be premenstrual. I've lost count of the number of times I've burst into tears, or shouted at my partner, only to realize with a shock a couple of hours later that I had PMT. It'll help you maintain a better grip on your emotions.
- If your PMT is unbearable and getting worse, visit your doctor. There is a small risk of endometriosis associated with heavy periods or extreme PMT, so it's best to get checked out.
- The contraceptive pill can help, although it may take some time for you to find one that suits you.

Case Study

Hannah, 29, suffered extreme mood swings after being prescribed the combination pill.

When I was 25, I was prescribed the brand Cileste. I was in a stable relationship at the time and wanted a hassle-free type of contraception. I visited my local GP, and after a five-minute consultation was prescribed Cileste. Within three weeks I began to feel very flat and experienced extreme tiredness. I went back to the doctor, who changed my prescription to another oestrogen pill.

The positive side-effects I was told to expect, such as light and pain-free periods, were non-existent. Instead, I experienced extremely swollen, tender breasts, headaches, and a feeling of being constantly on the verge of tears.

Within three months of starting the pill, I was in a full-blown state of depression. I was constantly tired with hapharzard sleep patterns and my appetite was inconsistent. I was also an emotional wreck: I became withdrawn from my friends and my boyfriend broke up with me. I felt that somebody had taken over my body.

Around this time one of my friends gave me the wake-up call that I needed. She actually yelled at me, in an attempt to shake me out of my emotional state. She convinced me to go to my GP and talk about my depression. I researched my symptoms on the Internet and was shocked to read that my emotions could be caused by the pill. I was put on a progestergen-only pill, was recommended to adjust my diet and to take a daily vitamin B6 supplement. After six months there was still no marked change, so I decided to stop taking the pill altogether.

I'm now in a relationship with a guy who was very supportive of me during this time. He knows why I can't take the pill, so we use condoms and are very careful. Although he doesn't mind using condoms, he does sometimes say that he doesn't feel as close to me because of it, but he knows that the other alternative is to have me in constant tears! I think that the pill is prescribed too easily and that side-effects aren't fully explained. I've been through 12 months of hell, but have come out the other side now. I have a good job, a fantastic boyfriend and my social life is just as busy as it used to be. But I'd never go back on the pill again, the benefits just aren't worth it.

The menopause

Early menopause

Typically, women go through the menopause between 47 and 53 years of age. However, an increasing number of women are experiencing early menopause as early as 26 years of age, which can be the cause of extreme unhappiness. '*Premature menopause basically means that your ovaries aren't working as they should, and are shutting down before their time*', says Dr Peter Bowen-Simpkins, a consultant gynaecologist, trustee and spokesperson for WellBeing of Women, a charity which funds vital health research into women's reproductive health. '*If you go through menopause before this age, you would be diagnosed with premature, or early menopause. If you miss a period and you're not pregnant, then you should immediately visit your doctor and request a Follicle Stimulating Hormone (FSH) test*', he says.

An FSH test calculates, from a blood test, the levels of hormones present in your body. An FSH will indicate whether your levels are normal. If the results are above 30, you've had ovarian failure and will no longer menstruate. You've actually gone through the menopause.

Another tell-tale sign of early menopause is hot flushes. Most of us are aware of this symptom from our mothers, but experiencing them at a young age is unusual. Hot flushes usually start with a hot, prickly feeling in the middle of the back, followed by a heatwave that envelops the back, chest, neck, face and scalp. Your temperature actually increases by up to eight degrees during a hot flush. Many women also find that they suffer from vaginal dryness, insomnia, heart palpitations, headaches, breast tenderness and weight gain. Although each woman is different, if you find that you suffer from just two early menopause symptoms, visit your GP to discuss your concerns.

Treatment for menopause

The most common form of treatment for menopause is hormone replacement therapy (HRT). However, for many women, HRT only exacerbates their symptoms. '*Women need to realize that menopause, early or otherwise, is not the end of the world*', says Maryon Stewart, founder of the Natural Health Advisory Service. When women go through the menopause, it can be a wake-up call for their overall health and lifestyle.

Menopause food recovery plan

A certain level of nutrients is necessary to enable the brain to balance out menopausal moods. Eliminate alcohol, hot drinks and spicy foods from your diet and replace them with protein, fruit, salads, nuts, seeds and regular snacks. Early menopausal women should also eliminate brown bread from their diet as this can impede nutrients in the system.

- Eat around 100g of isoflavones per day. Isoflavones are a source of the naturally occurring plant oestrogen, which helps to replace this lost hormone in the body.
- Take linseed, soya and red clover supplements on a daily basis.
- Exercise and relaxation are also important – aim for around four to five physical sessions a week. Exercise to the point of breathlessness. Try dancing, walking or anything that fits into your everyday life.

GP check! Hypothyroidism

Depression can result from hypothyroidism. Up to 20 per cent of all cases of chronic depression may be associated with low production of thyroid hormones. A University of North Carolina study found that among women with mildly decreased thyroid function, the number who had suffered depression at least once in their lives was almost three times that of women with normal thyroid function (56 per cent versus 20 per cent). Often, unfortunately, patients who are treated for depression are not first given thyroid tests.

Case Study

Nicky Hoffman, 41, is a company secretary who lives in Marden, Kent. She started the menopause at the age of 30.

Ever since I was a teenager I'd had problems with my periods. I'd not only have heavy periods for around eight days every month, but I'd have breakthrough bleeding as well. As my two children had been born and my husband and I had decided to not have any more children, I had decided to take my GP's advice and have a hysterectomy.

My gynaecologist warned me that there was a chance that I could go through the menopause early, but I assumed that this meant it might be during my late 40s. About six months after the hysterectomy, I began having night sweats, anxiety attacks and my breasts were very tender. Worse, though, were the mood swings. I was constantly depressed and began to believe that I was going crazy. I didn't know how to ask for help, as I couldn't explain how I felt. After about six months of these symptoms, I visited my GP and listed all my symptoms. I was shocked when I was told that I was going through the menopause. I was put on HRT, but this only made my symptoms worse. My breasts became tender and my mood swings became worse.

Finally, after four years of putting up with this situation, I read about the Daisy Network, which is an advisory service for women under the age of 40 who have gone through the menopause. I can't describe the relief I felt to talk to women who were going through the exact same situation as me. I visited a nutritionist through the Daisy Network. I was told to eliminate caffeine, sugar and wheat from my diet, and began taking St John's wort, fish oils and Aria, which is a natural source of isoflavones. As there's a higher risk of osteoporosis once you hit the menopause, I make sure that my diet includes calcium, and I walk or go to the gym every day. Within one month the difference was amazing. I still occasionally had night sweats and had a few moody episodes, but they were no worse than PMT.

After six months, all my symptoms had disappeared and my husband couldn't believe that he finally had his wife back. It's now 11 years since I began the menopause, and I'm the happiest and healthiest I've ever been. I'm very conscious of my body and my health. If something doesn't feel right, I immediately adjust my diet, because I know how important it is to look after myself.

Part 2
Happy Food

Happy Food

We've all heard the saying 'you are what you eat'. So what does your diet say about you? Do you pile your plate high with fresh, nutritious fruit and vegetables, bursting with colour and health? Or do you grab ready-made meals and eat on the run, paying little or no attention to what you put in your stomach? Our busy, frantic lives can leave us feeling stressed, tired, irritable, grumpy and depressed, with little time to prepare meals. We're too tired to exercise, too busy to cook properly and even too tired to get a decent night's sleep.

It's no wonder, then, that most of the time we end up eating ready-made meals in front of the television. We know that this sort of diet can play havoc with our waistlines, but this pales in comparison with what it can do to our emotional and mental health.

Food and endorphins

When you eat a meal, the contents of it are absorbed into your bloodstream. If the meal is a healthy one, say a dish of grilled chicken and steamed vegetables, your body will utilize the nutrients and goodness from the food.

However, when we skip breakfast, gulp down a store-bought sandwich at lunchtime or eat a carbohydrate-heavy dinner (accompanied by several glasses of wine), we are depriving our bodies of much-needed nutrients. These nutrients, while necessary for our overall health, are also essential to creating good moods by enabling the body to produce the endorphins serotonin and norepinephrine. Instead, our diets are high in toxic mood foods: sweets, starches and fats, not to mention alcohol, nicotine and caffeine. The greatest mood food enemies are wheat, soy, sugar and fats: not only do they lack any positive mood vitamins, but they actually rob the body of nutrients, making you feel even worse than before.

What you eat – and when you eat it – has a remarkable effect on your moods, energy and motivation. In this chapter, we'll learn all about what to eat, when to eat it, and most importantly, which foods to avoid.

Foods and moods

- A person eats a high-protein snack, such as prawn salad or turkey sandwich.
- Blood levels of amino acids (including tryptophan) then rise.
- All blood acids compete for entry into the brain.
- Low amounts of tryptophan enter the brain.
- Only moderate amounts of serotonin are made and stored.
- A person feels depressed, irritable, or craves a carbohydrate-rich snack

Eating a protein-rich meal lowers brain tryptophan and serotonin levels while eating a carbohydrate-rich snack raises them. As we've seen in Part 1, tryptophan is a large amino acid that shares an entry gate into the brain with several other large amino acids, such as tyrosine, and which manufactures serotonin. When you eat a protein-rich meal, you flood the blood with both tryptophan and its competing amino acids, and they fight for entry into the brain. Tryptophan gets crowded out, and only a small amount gets through the blood-brain barrier. As a result, serotonin levels do not rise noticeably after a meal or snack that contains protein, even if that food is high in tryptophan.

On the other hand, a carbohydrate-rich meal triggers the release of insulin from the pancreas. Insulin causes most amino acids floating in the blood to be absorbed into the body's cells, all except tryptophan, which remains in the bloodstream at relatively high levels. With its competitors removed, tryptophan can freely enter the brain, causing serotonin levels to rise. This high level of serotonin increases feelings of calm, improves sleep patterns, increases pain tolerance and reduces cravings for carbohydate-rich foods. This doesn't mean you can gorge on bread and pasta. The secret is to eat complex, slow-releasing carbohydrates to get the feel-good benefits over a longer period of time. (See GI foods on page 73 for a more comprehensive explanation.)

The other main mood enhancer is norepinephrine, which is made from the amino acid tyrosine. The body makes these particular endorphins from the food we eat and therefore we can, to a certain extent, raise the level of these substances in the brain by eating specific foods. Many foods we recommend as happy foods are high in protein. Scientifically, food has been shown to have a significant effect on raising your mood only if the levels of serotonin or norepinephrine in your body are low before you eat. It is not a question of the more you eat, the happier you become, but more a question reversing a negative feeling that has been caused by a low serotonin or norepinephrine level.

The main sources of endorphins are sugary and simple carbohydrate-rich foods. You may have noticed that after an afternoon treat of sweets, cakes, biscuits or chocolate, you feel happier and more energetic. The problem with eating these foods to improve your moods or increase your energy is that they are very rapidly absorbed into the bloodstream. The sudden influx of sugar causes a serotonin rush – so you'll immediately feel 'picked up' – but the secondary effect is a rapid production of insulin. Insulin breaks down sugar so that the body can absorb it. If there is a sudden rise in the sugar level in the blood the insulin quickly breaks it down, leading to a drop in both sugar and endorphin levels. This leaves you feeling even lower (physically and emotionally) than before. (See GI foods on page 73 for a fuller explanation of insulin and energy levels).

Monitoring your endorphin levels

Women are particularly sensitive to changes in sugar and insulin levels, and hence endorphin levels, and may experience extreme reactions. Swings in endorphin levels can result in feeling agitated, moody and aggressive. If this sounds like you, keep a diary of everything you eat and your resulting mood, to help you determine which foods are a contributing factor to your low moods. After one month of keeping your diary, take time to consider the effects certain foods have on your moods and energy levels. Try eliminating all suspect foods from your diet for four weeks, and again, keep a diary and chart your emotional and energy reactions. After four weeks, slowly reintroduce these foods into your diet and note any effects.

Food allergies

Could a food allergy be causing your unhappiness?

Food allergies can be responsible for many symptoms, especially digestive problems, from bloating to constipation, and diarrhoea to abdominal cramps. These are almost always accompanied by mental and physical symptoms, such as mood changes, chronic tiredness, depression, increased appetite, sleepiness after meals, inability to concentrate and a host of minor ailments from itches and rashes to asthma and sinus problems.

Complete this instant allergy check to discover whether you may have a food allergy or intolerance. If you answer 'yes' to more than one answer you may have an allergy.

- Do you gain weight in hours?
- Do you get bloated after eating?
- Do you suffer from diarrhoea or constipation?
- Do you suffer from abdominal pain?
- Do you sometimes get really sleepy after eating?
- Do you suffer from hay fever?
- Do you suffer from rashes, itches, asthma or shortness of breath?
- Do you suffer from water retention?
- Do you suffer from other aches or pains, from time to time, possibly after eating certain foods?
- Do you get better on holidays abroad, when your diet is completely different?

Discover the culprit

Do you hanker after pasta or white bread around the time your period is due? It may seem odd, but often the foods a person is allergic to are those which they crave. One of the physical symptoms of an allergic reaction can be a sudden fluctuation in blood sugar levels, which, in turn, affects the appetite. About 1 per cent of the UK population has a food allergy, although it's believed that around one in three people suffer food sensitivities.

A food sensitivity may occur immediately after you've eaten a certain foodstuff or some time after. For example, you may eat a piece of toast for breakfast, only to feel groggy, irritable and emotionally unwell shortly afterwards. Or, your diet may be so carbohydrate-heavy that you have a general feeling of sleepiness and negativity. You may also find that you suffer from mild diarrhoea or, conversely, that some foods make constipation worse.

A food sensitivity or intolerance occurs when the body has difficulty digesting a particular food and therefore reacts against it. In normal digestion the foods we eat are broken down into their specific parts. Nutrients are absorbed into the bloodstream through the digestive tract, and are then utilized by the body for energy and nourishment. Anything left over is flushed through the bowel.

However, if the foods are not properly broken down because of some digestive malfunction then the body will either not be able to absorb them properly or, since they have not been properly 'processed', may react against them. If you think you could have a food allergy, ask your GP for a referral to an allergy clinic.

One of the most basic ways to feel happier and more energetic is through eating healthy, well-balanced meals. When you're feeling down and listless, it's unlikely that you'll have the energy or motivation to concoct three nutritionally balanced meals each day. The result? You end up in a no-win situation. This is where a daily multivitamin can help, particularly one formulated for women. This at least can help temporarily bridge the nutritional gap existing in your body. See pages 48–59 for more information on vitamins and minerals.

Wheat warning

The most common allergen is wheat, so if you know – or think – that you're allergic or sensitive to wheat, eliminate it completely from your diet. You can still indulge in alternative options, such as rye bread, rice cakes, oat cakes, rye crackers, oatmeal porridge, corn/rice/vegetable pasta, rice noodles, brown rice, quinoa, corn, potato, sweet potato, polenta or millet.

Happy and sad foods

Now that we know why it's important to eat healthy, nutritious food, we can look at which foods come under this umbrella. Anything in its natural state, such as fresh vegetables, fruit, nuts or seeds, are, in most cases, unprocessed and untouched, so they contain the largest amounts of 'happy' nutrients. Many other foods, which are slightly removed from their natural state, such as oats, meat, chicken and fish, have been handled, but are still relatively close to their original form. These are the foods to stock up on, as they're relatively devoid of chemicals (particularly if organic) and are full of natural, mood-enhancing goodness.

We all know that a fatty, stodgy meal of burger and chips is unlikely to inspire us to want to get up and run five miles around the park. On the other hand, a breakfast of fresh fruit salad, organic yoghurt and pumpkin seeds provides a virtuous and wholesome start to the day. The difference between these two meals is in the nutrients they contain and hence, the way they can affect how the body's physical functions and emotional moods.

Good mood foods

Brown rice	Good replacement for pasta or potatoes
Fish	Contains high levels of omega-3 fatty acids (low levels can cause feelings of depression)
Garlic	Gives you energy and is ideal for boosting immunity
Ginger	Helps fight colds and flu
Berries	Packed full of antioxidants
Oats	Researchers say that eating a bowl of porridge is not only filling, but that the properties in oats are the best weapon against winter blues
Mustard	Good for treating muscular pain and sustaining body warmth
Water	Healthier alternative to that comforting cup of tea or coffee during the colder months. It's important to keep up your daily intake of 2 litres (3½ pints) of water throughout the year.

Bad mood foods

Caffeine	Although coffee, fizzy drinks and sugary foods may make you feel immediately better, your feelings of depression will only increase afterwards. This is because after the 'high', the 'low' that follows will lower your spirits even more. Try herbal or decaffeinated teas and choose organic or dark organic chocolate in small quantities.
Alcohol	While it's tempting to spend the long winter nights in the pub, over-indulging in alcohol will only make you feel worse, as it robs your body of vitamin B. Vitamin B is necessary for a healthy, well-balanced nervous system.
Fatty foods	It may be comforting to tuck into some stodgy foods, but fatty foods will only increase your feelings of lethargy.

A–Z of top mood foods

Almonds

Happy ingredients Vitamin A, vitamin B, calcium, magnesium, phosphorus, potassium, oleic acid

Why they're good for you Almonds contain calcium, which researchers say can help to ease mood swings, depression, irritability and even bloating. The magnesium and potassium also work together to help stabilize your mood.

Happy tip Eating a handful of almonds every day can help you lose weight or control your current measurements, say researchers.

Apples

Happy ingredients Vitamin C, vitamin E, malic and tartaric acid, pectin

Why they're good for you Yes, an apple a day keeps the doctor away, but it also keeps you off the therapist's couch. Apples help boost your digestion, which means that even if you do feel blue, your digestion system will be working away, removing toxins from your body. And it's difficult to feel down, physically, mentally and emotionally, if your body is pure and sparkling.

Happy tip Sniff an apple. The aroma can help to calm your frazzled nerves and induce a feeling of tranquillity.

Apricots

Happy ingredients Vitamin A, vitamin B, vitamin C, iron, magnesium, manganese, phosphorus, potassium, natural sugars

Why they're good for you Apricots have a balancing effect on your nervous system, as the iron, magnesium and potassium all help to calm stressed, frayed nerves. The antioxidant effects of vitamins A and C will also keep your immune system in tip-top shape, while the presence of vitamin C will ensure that your brain receives feel-good messages.

Happy tip If you're menstruating, try eating a handful of dried apricots or adding fresh apricots to your morning muesli. The vitamin B may help to reduce period pain.

Bananas

Happy ingredients Vitamin B, vitamin C, magnesium, potassium, lutein, fibre
Why they're good for you Vitamin B and magnesium help the menstruating body to function healthily, reduce sugar cravings and soothe swollen ankles, fingers and bellies. The potassium helps to reduce cramps. Bananas are ideal for those late-afternoon energy dips.
Happy tip Avoid eating over-ripe bananas. Their energy-giving properties are released too quickly into your bloodstream, so you may feel just as flat and lethargic only half an hour after eating one.

Beans

Happy ingredients Fibre, iron, folic acid, phytochemicals
Why they're good for you A near-perfect health food, beans are high in carbohydrates, fibre, iron and folic acid, yet contain little or no fat and no cholesterol. Beans are one of the best sources of soluble fibre, which helps to stabilize blood sugar. Eaten alongside meat or dairy products, this is an ideal food to help keep your energy levels balanced.
Happy tip The zinc in beans is a great way to increase energy and lift a low mood. Try to include a serving of beans during your period, as it'll give you a much-needed boost.

Beetroot

Happy ingredients Potassium, folic acid, fibre
Why it's good for you Research has shown that people who suffer from depression, or low moods, tend to be deficient in folic acid. Introducing beetroot into your diet will help boost your folic acid levels. Beetroot is a favourite of naturopaths, owing to its excellent healing qualities. The many nutrients and vitamins in beetroot stimulate the liver, kidneys, gall bladder, spleen and bowel, as well as strengthening the immune system. Chinese acupuncturists believe that keeping these areas strong and healthy will ensure that your energy levels stay strong and your outlook positive.
Happy tip Low energy can be associated with poor kidney function. Try juicing one raw beetroot with two carrots for your morning drink. You will feel happier and your skin and eyes will be clear and sparkling too.

Blueberries

Happy ingredients Vitamin A/betacarotene, vitamin B1, vitamin E, vitamin C, potassium, quercitin, soluble fibre, cellulose

Why they're good for you Recently hailed as 'wonderfoods', blueberries are certainly one fruit that deserve their long-awaited publicity. First, the health angle: blueberries contain massive amounts of antioxidants, so eating a handful of fresh or frozen blueberries every day can help to slow the ageing process, protect against heart disease and many types of cancer. Secondly, antioxidants help to boost the immune system, so you'll be less likely to feel the overwhelming effects of stress and overwork. Plus, they're packed full of vitamin C, which helps to convert tryptophan into serotonin – the feel-good chemical.

Happy tip As well as blueberries, add raspberries, blackberries and strawberries to your daily menu.

Celery

Happy ingredients Vitamin A/betacarotene, vitamin B1, vitamin C, vitamin E, calcium, potassium, fibre

Why it's good for you Celery is probably most often eaten as part of a calorie-controlled diet. Nonetheless, celery has many other beneficial properties. It helps to detoxify the kidneys, so you'll be less likely to suffer from a 'dragging' feeling. Celery also has a high water content; research has shown that dehydration can contribute to irritability and moodiness.

Happy tip Add celery to your morning juice – it's a good way to neutralize your ingredients.

Eggs

Happy ingredients Sodium, selenium, iron, zinc, vitamin A, vitamin B

Why they're good for you Eggs get a bad press due to their high cholesterol content, but they are an excellent source of protein, vitamins, minerals and unsaturated fats. Of the 5g (0.2oz) of fat in an egg, ten times as much is monounsaturated (like in olive oil) than is cholesterol, which actually helps lower the risk of heart disease. We need some cholesterol for a healthy brain and in order to make sex and stress hormones.

Happy tip Try scrambled eggs on rye toast for a healthy and happy start to the day. Eggs and rye bread are slow-releasing, so you'll be fuller for longer and less likely to need a mid-morning snack.

Lettuce

Happy ingredients Vitamin A/betacarotene, vitamin C, folic acid, calcium, iron, potassium, fibre

Why it's good for you There are several varieties of lettuce, including butterhead, lollo rosso and iceberg, all of which are high in nutrients and low in calories. Opt for the darker varieties, as they contain more antioxidant vitamins than lighter types. The iron, vitamin C and vitamin A/betacarotene in lettuce helps to stabilize energy levels and support the body in making good mood chemicals. Owing to their high water content, lettuces offer an ideal means of staying hydrated. They are a source of calcium and folate, both of which have been shown to help stabilize moods. Lettuce should be a daily inclusion in your diet.

Happy tip Can't get to sleep? Lettuce contains a natural sedative called lactucarium. If eaten just before bedtime, lettuce helps ward off insomnia and aids restful sleep.

Linseeds

Happy ingredients Calcium, magnesium, zinc, fibre, omega-3 fat, omega-6 fat

Why they're good for you Linseeds (or flax seeds) are one of the richest plant sources of omega-3 fat (nearly 60 per cent of their total fat content). As your brain is comprised of more than 60 per cent fat, it requires some fat from the diet in order to function correctly. Omega-3 is a member of the unsaturated fat family that is most often lacking in the diet (members of this family are also found in fish oils). The Omega-3 fat from linseeds is incorporated into cell membranes, helping to maintain their efficient functioning. Linseeds are also a rich source of soluble fibre, which helps keep the bowel moving and well cleansed.

Happy tip Sprinkle a handful of linseeds on your morning muesli for a happy way to start the day.

Milk and cheese

Happy ingredients Vitamin A/betacarotene, vitamin B1, vitamin B2, vitamin D, calcium, protein

Why they're good for you Calcium, one of the most important nutrients found in dairy foods, is needed for women's overall health and wellbeing. Between the ages of 30 and 40, women should take around 700mg a day to ensure optimum development of bones, teeth and other tissues. Dairy foods also contain the all-important vitamin D, which the body needs to absorb calcium in the diet. Milk and cheese provide vitamins B1 and B2, which help the body maximize the energy obtained from foods. B-complex vitamins help to prevent cracks and sores forming around the mouth, boost energy levels and combat premenstrual syndrome. Milk and cheese are good sources of vitamin A (which in dairy products is called retinol), an essential skin nutrient that helps wounds to heal and aids good skin hydration.

Happy tip Calcium is one of the main promoters of happiness and a small piece of your favourite cheese each day is a great mood boost.

Oats

Happy ingredients Vitamin B, vitamin E, iron, zinc

Why they're good for you Oats are a remarkably versatile grain with wide-ranging health properties. As well as being a good source of carbohydrates, they are high in both soluble and insoluble fibre. This means they are digested slowly, so don't raise blood sugar dramatically, which keeps mood and energy levels up for a while after eating. The fibre in oats contributes to a healthy gut – not just keeping you regular but also binding waste products. Studies have shown that oats also help lower cholesterol. Herbalists recommend oat extracts to help calm anxiety and depression. Oats are loaded with B vitamins, vitamin E and important minerals such as iron and zinc. All of these make for a healthy nervous system and much, more.

Happy tip If you suffer from Seasonal Affective Disorder (SAD), eat a bowl of porridge each morning for breakfast. Studies have shown that those who eat porridge on a regular basis are less likely to suffer from SAD.

Oily fish

Happy ingredients Omega-3 fat, omega-6 fat

Why it's good for you Researchers have found, through worldwide studies, that as fish consumption increases, depression rates go down. Try to eat fish at least three times a week, concentrating on sardines, mackerel, anchovies, salmon, tuna, oysters, scallops, mussels and crab. See the section on omega-3 and omega-6 fats on pages 68–69 for more information on the benefits of eating fish.

Happy tip Tuck into a salmon or tuna salad for a mood lift – the omega-3s will boost your serotonin levels.

Peas

Happy ingredients Vitamin B1, vitamin C, folate, calcium, iron, potassium, zinc, protein, fibre

Why they're good for you Peas help wounds heal, aid digestion, help prevent white spots on nails, heart disease, insomnia, thinning hair and exhaustion. Peas (English, garden, mangetout, sugar snap, black-eyed) are an excellent addition to the diet because they supply essential nutrients in abundance. They are particularly rich in protein, normally gained from meats or dairy foods, so are especially important for vegans and vegetarians. Peas are digested slowly and only gradually absorbed into the bloodstream. This is good news for people with diabetes (both insulin- and non-insulin-dependent forms). By eating peas and other pulses (such as beans, lentils and kidney beans) on a regular basis, diabetics can help regulate their blood sugar levels. Peas are one of the richest sources of vitamin B1, a lack of which can cause extreme tiredness, anxiety and loss of appetite. Black-eyed peas contain folate (a form of folic acid), necessary for a healthy nervous system.

Happy tip Try making a batch of pea soup and storing it in the freezer. On grey, winter days, the richly coloured soup will cheer you up and help increase your daily intake of vegetables.

Pears

Happy ingredients Copper, iodine, magnesium, phosphorus, zinc, natural sugar, pectin

Why they're good for you Pears are extremely calming foods. As they contain large amounts of phosphorus and zinc, they help to lift your mood. The natural sugars will also help to balance out your sugar levels, so keeping your mood and energy levels constant.

Happy tip Try making a concoction of apple and pear juice in the morning. Your bowels will feel the benefits and you'll be unlikely to experience an energy lull until it's time for lunch.

Quinoa

Happy ingredients Amino acids, potassium, magnesium, zinc, iron, vitamin B group

Why it's good for you In its native Latin America, quinoa (pronounced keen-wa) means 'mother' in the Quechua language, showing its immense significance both nutritionally and spiritually. It's not technically a grain, but a seed, which contains significant amounts of mono- and polyunsaturated fats. Quinoa also contains much more protein than other grain-like foods, which helps make it a very sustaining basis for a meal. It contains the full range of essential amino acids including the all-important tryptophan, not to mention its high content of the minerals potassium, magnesium, zinc and iron. Quinoa provides a spectrum of B vitamins, including pantothenic acid or vitamin B5, which is essential for the adrenal glands to mount a healthy response to stress.

Happy tip Try making your morning porridge with quinoa instead of oats.

Sesame seeds

Happy ingredients Vitamin B1, vitamin B3, vitamin B6, folic acid, calcium, magnesium, selenium, zinc, omega-6 fat

Why they're good for you Sesame seeds lend a delicious flavour to foods. Unfortunately, because they are so small, they often pass through the body undigested, which means their nutrient content is missed. However, when chewed thoroughly, or used as a paste (such as tahini) or oil, they provide a rich source of the fats that are important for a healthy nervous system. Sesame seeds contain powerful antioxidants such as selenium and zinc, which help to counteract the negative physical and emotional effects that stress can have on the body. They're also rich in B vitamins, which are important for sustaining steady energy release and hormone production.

Happy tip Try sprinkling sesame seeds on your salmon or tuna salad. They're a perfect accompaniment, and a good combination to boost serotonin and relax your nerves.

Sunflower seeds

Happy ingredients Vitamin B1, vitamin B3, vitamin B6, vitamin E, calcium, magnesium, selenium, zinc, omega-6 fat

Why they're good for you These little seeds from the studded centre of the beautiful yellow flowers are powerhouses of nutrients. The omega-6 and monounsaturated fats and the vitamin E in them help minimize heart disease as well as boost the elasticity of skin. Sunflower seeds and sesame seeds (see opposite) are rich in calcium and magnesium, important for relaxation and contraction of the muscles (including the heart) and bone health. Magnesium is needed for each cell to produce energy, yet it is also considered the 'calming' mineral. The zinc and selenium in sunflower seeds (as well as other chemicals such as sesamol) are important antioxidants. Low levels of zinc are associated with poor immunity, infertility, bad skin and depression. The vitamin B5 in the seeds is essential for a healthy response to stress.

Happy tip Keep a small bag of sunflower seeds in your bag to snack on whenever you're peckish. You'll increase your daily amount of good fats and oils without even trying.

Turkey and chicken

Happy ingredients Sodium, niacin, vitamin B6, phosphorus, selenium, zinc

Why they're good for you Most people associate roast turkey with Christmas. After a generous helping of this yummy white meat, you will usually feel satiated, sleepy and content. And for good reason – skinless turkey breast is about the leanest meat there is, so it's an excellent source of protein with one portion giving you as much as half your daily requirement. Organic, free-range chicken is also good and both meats contain the amino acid tryptophan, which the body converts to serotonin. Turkey and chicken provide good doses of B vitamins, needed to make energy and respond to stress. These lean meats are also rich in zinc. Eating protein such as turkey or chicken makes a meal more satisfying for longer, helping to keep energy, moods and concentration levels more even. Chickens and turkeys are usually reared intensively, so choose organic.

Happy tip A chicken sandwich is a great bed-time snack, as the tryptophan in the chicken not only encourages a good night's sleep, but helps you wake up in a good mood, too.

Walnuts

Happy ingredients Vitamin E, magnesium, manganese, zinc, fibre, omega-3 fat, omega-6 fat, monounsaturated fat

Why they're good for you Walnuts are the richest nut source of omega-3 fat, which is sadly lacking in most diets today. They also contain zinc, a must-have nutrient, necessary for good mental and emotional health. When your body is stressed, it requires zinc to help it function correctly. When levels of zinc become low, you may experience anxiety and depression.

Happy tip Keep a bag of walnuts in your handbag at all times. They're a great afternoon pick-me-up.

Yoghurt

Happy ingredients Vitamin A/betacarotene, vitamin B1, vitamin B2, vitamin B3, vitamin D, calcium, magnesium, phosphorus, potassium, zinc

Why it's good for you Ever since cows were first domesticated, humans have been eating fermented milk and its benefits have long been recognized. Yoghurt is made by adding *lactobacillus* and *bifidobacteria* cultures to milk, but some are pasteurised after the culture is added (killing it off), so it's important to buy 'live' yoghurts. Live bacteria are well known as vital inhabitants of our digestive tracts where they help to maintain the correct acidity, enhance immunity and help with digestion. Yoghurt is a good source of protein, particularly for vegetarians, and makes a quick breakfast food. It contains tryptophan, which the body needs to make the mood-booster, serotonin. Some people who react badly to milk products are fine with yoghurt because the bacteria ferment it by eating the milk sugar (lactose), making it more digestible. Yoghurt, like all milk produce, is a rich source of calcium, which is not only needed for healthy bones, but also the proper contraction and relaxation of muscles and for the nerves to fire their messages efficiently.

Happy tip The protein in yoghurt helps to boost tryptophan. Try eating a small tub of low-fat yoghurt every day.

Happy meal ideas

Breakfast
Bowl of porridge
Carrot and apple juice
Herbal tea such as peppermint or lemon

Lunch
Grilled chicken, romaine lettuce, snow peas, mushrooms
with lemon juice dressing salad

Dinner
Salmon steaks with sesame seed crusts

Snacks
Dried fruit such as figs, apricots or prunes
Fruit rich in vitamin C, such as oranges or kiwi fruit
Sunflower or pumpkin seeds

Liquid intake
Drink at least 2 litres (3½ pints) of water per day. Invest in a water filter:
it's cheaper than bottled water and at least you know it's fresh!

Herbs for happiness

Herbs have been used for centuries, not only for flavour in cooking, but as natural remedies too. Try ginger to lift the spirits, cinnamon to counteract exhaustion, camomile (usually drunk as tea) to help with nervous tension and peppermint to help calm nerves and relieve anger. Basil is thought to clarify the mind, so try a large dollop of fresh pesto stirred through pasta to get your mind ready for some serious concentration.

Rosemary
Contains Vitamin C, vitamin E, folic acid, carotenes, iron
What it does This beautifully scented herb is ideal for lifting your mood, so helping to relieve stress and anxiety. Rosemary also stimulates the circulatory and nervous system, allowing the body and mind to relax and function in a normal, healthy way. Don't use or eat if pregnant.

Camomile
Contains Vitamin C, vitamin E, folic acid, vitamin A/betacarotene, calcium, iron, magnesium

What it does This pretty, daisy-like flower is rich in calcium, magnesium and iron, which are vital for healthy skin. It helps prevent pale skin, brittle nails, dry hair, stress, insomnia, constipation and indigestion. The iron present in camomile aids production of haemoglobin – the red pigment in blood cells, which transports oxygen to the tissues. The oils in the camomile flower (apigenin and azulene) calm the nervous system, relax the digestive tract, speed up the healing process and fight disease.

Sage
Contains Vitamin C, vitamin E, folic acid, vitamin A/betacarotene, iron
What it does Aids digestion, treats acne, fights cellulite. The Latin name for sage, *Salvia*, can be translated as 'healing plant'. Sage helps the central nervous system by increasing circulation and helping to improve digestion.

Thyme
Contains Vitamin C, vitamin E, folic acid, vitamin A/betacarotene, iron
What it does Anti-ageing, combats headaches, insomnia, stress. Thyme contains antioxidants, so it's useful to help maintain a healthy nervous system. A cup of cold thyme tea is recommended for tension headaches.

Basil
Contains Vitamin C, vitamin E, folic acid, vitamin A/betacarotene, iron
What it does Relieves migraine, stress, flatulence, cramps and nausea, prevents dry skin and brittle nails. The fragrance of basil has a mood-enhancing effect. Basil can also relieve migraine and stomach cramps.

Garlic
Contains Folate, allicin, iron, magnesium, selenium, sodium, potassium, zinc
What it does Boosts circulation and immunity. Its main benefit is its ability to improve circulation, enhancing the flow of nutrients and oxygen to the extremities. Garlic contains sulphurous compounds that help the body resist colds, flu and other infections, so if you're prone to winter colds and flu, try to include garlic in as many meals as possible. The sulphurous compounds also stimulate the liver and act as a detoxifier, helping to rid the body of any toxins, which can contribute to a low mood.

Water

Water truly is nature's greatest health booster – and best of all, it's free! While you can survive for up to a week without food, you could only survive for about two days without making up fluid lost from the body. Considering that the body is composed of 75 per cent water, it is surprising to think that you only need to drink around 1.5 litres (3 pints) of water each day to keep your body well supplied. Water is necessary for all bodily processes: to flush toxins through your liver and kidneys; to help pump oxygen through your body; and to keep your skin smooth and supple.

Water and the liver

If you think of the liver as your very own cleansing system, you'll realize how important it is to take care of it. The liver is responsible for neutralising the toxins and wastes produced in the body as a result of the breakdown of, for example, fatty foods and alcohol. If you've been eating unhealthy foods and drinking too much alcohol, you may feel lethargic and generally 'under the weather'. In part, this is because you have been putting your liver under too much pressure and it is unable to continue processing toxins at its optimum rate. Drinking plenty of water supports the liver's cleansing function, by flushing out waste before it accumulates.

Water and the kidneys

The kidneys play a similar role to that of the liver – filtering and neutralizing bodily wastes. The kidneys do this by removing waste products from the blood, diluting them with water and flushing them out of the body. However, this delicate balance is easily upset. For example, a high salt intake in the diet encourages the kidneys to reabsorb too much water, which may lead to fluid retention, tiredness, lethargy and puffy-looking skin. Coffee and alcohol act as diuretics, encouraging excess water loss via the urine, which can lead to dehydration.

Tap, filtered or mineral?

There is much research over which is the healthiest source of drinking water. Tap water is probably the closest to being a 'processed' source, as it usually has chlorine, flouride and aluminium sulphate added during purification. Research shows that the chemicals added during this process provide few, if any health benefits. Using a water jug with a carbon filter removes any added chemicals, but allows the naturally occurring minerals that are beneficial to health to pass through. Distilled water is certainly the purest form of water, devoid of any impurities and other negative elements such as lead, flouride, chlorine and pesticides. However, drinking only distilled water may mean that your body misses out on some of the important minerals present in other waters.

Many people today drink bottled water, assuming that they are providing their body with the healthiest form of fluid available. However, bottled water can come in many forms: variously labelled natural mineral water, spring water and table water. Some of these terms have no legal significance and do not necessarily mean that the water is free of impurities. Some may have been bottled from sources such as lakes, rivers and even municipal water supplies. If you are unsure about which type to buy, look for the words 'natural mineral water'. This indicates that the water has not been processed in any way and is of a high standard.

Water for health

If you regularly suffer from the '3pm slump', it is likely that you try to overcome this mid-afternoon spell of tiredness with caffeine or a sugary or fatty snack. This may initially revive you, but within the hour you will feel tired again, perhaps with a headache and even slightly nauseous. Instead of snacking, try drinking a large glass of water or eating a juicy piece of fruit, such as an orange, an apple or some grapes. You'll immediately feel the benefits of rehydrating your body and mind and will be less likely to suffer another energy slump.

Regular exercise is good for you but rapidly increases water loss. It is possible to lose 1 litre (almost 2 pints) of water during a hard workout, so ensure that you have a bottle of water nearby to keep your fluid levels topped up.

Happy tip

If you're drinking your prescribed eight glasses of filtered water every day of the working week, make sure you continue at the weekend. Feeling low and irritable at the weekend can be caused by dehydration. If you're used to drinking a cup of tea at 7.30 every workday morning, do the same at the weekends. Your body is used to this caffeine hit, and doing without can cause feelings of withdrawal, such as sluggishness and irritability.

10 rules for happy meals

1. Drink at least 2 litres (3½ pints) of water every day. Don't bother trying to count the number of glasses you drink, just keep a 2-litre bottle and refill this each morning.

2. Eat a rainbow diet. Pile your plate high with colourful foods. Anything red, yellow, orange or blue is high in serotonin-boosting antioxidants.

3. Remember the five-a-day rule. Eat at least five servings of fruit and vegetables. Make a start by juicing one carrot, one stick of celery, one pear, one apple and one kiwi fruit every morning. This actually counts as just three servings, according to guidelines published by the Food Standards Agency, but it's a great way to start the day and you won't need to worry about trying to cram in your daily fruit and vegetable intake at dinner time.)

4. Each plenty of fibre-rich foods, such as beans, lentils, whole grains, fruit and vegetables.

5. Make sure you have protein with every meal. Try yoghurt for breakfast, chicken with a lunchtime salad, meat or fish with vegetables at night.

6. Cut down on your drinking. Alcohol robs your body of mood-enhancing B vitamins. Drink no more that one or two units per day.

7. Eliminate processed foods such as white bread, white rice and white pasta from your diet. These are full of sugars that will just land you in a slump shortly after eating them.

8. Try to start each day with a cup of herbal tea or lemon and warm water.

9. Caffeine is your enemy! Try to restrict yourself to just one cup of tea or coffee each day.

10. Stop smoking – nothing changes your mood (for the worse) more rapidly than a hit of nicotine.

Food and your body clock

Have you ever wondered why you sometimes wake up exhausted, despite a solid nine hours' sleep? Or why you have trouble staying awake, let alone concentrating, in the early afternoon? Or why you're ravenous in the morning or evening, but rarely both? Well, the answer to all these questions lies in the secret of your internal body clock.

Your body clock, like every clock, has a cycle of 24 hours. During this time your body rests, detoxifies, restores cells and copes with the daily stresses and strains of everyday life. It's important then, that you provide your body with enough fuel to cope with all these actions.

If you skip meals, or overeat at separate meals, you override your body's natural ability to recognise hunger and fullness. This makes it difficult for your body to understand how much food it needs, and when. The end result can be bingeing or snacking heavily at odd times. So how can you make sure that you're eating the right food and at the right time?

Ernest Hilton, director of the Montignac method, which advocates eating high-protein, refined carbohydrate meals, believes it's important to listen to your body's needs. '*Eating regularly and evenly keeps your blood sugar levels even. These levels control the amount of energy you have, your mood and your weight*', says Mr Hilton. '*If you skip meals, you'll rock this ideal blood sugar level. Eating three meals at the same time every day is necessary as it keeps your blood sugar on a consistent level. If you eat less in one meal, you'll be likely to overeat in the next meal to compensate. Unfortunately, trying to play catch-up with your diet doesn't work. All you're doing is providing your body with food to store, not burn*', 'he says.

The secret of eating at the right time is to choose the correct type of foods for that particular time. And this depends on their respective glycaemic index, or GI, which is a clever term for explaining the amount of energy a food gives you and at what rate it does so. Foods that break down quickly, such as white rice, sweets and sugary cereals, have the highest GIs. These raise the blood sugar level quickly and increase cravings for more of the same. Foods with a low GI include sweet potatoes, cracked wheat, porridge, apples, yoghurt and lentils.

Plan your day

If you organize your meals to respond to your body's clock, then you'll keep energy levels up and maintain a feel-good mood throughout the day. Here's a typical daily menu designed to do this:

7:30am
Breakfast

Small glass of cranberry juice
Slice of melon
One thick slice of granary toast with 1 tbsp light cream cheese and 12 grilled cherry tomatoes
Tea, coffee or herbal tea

This is a good slow-releasing carbohydrate breakfast, which will give you the energy to start the day and ensure you're not hungry by lunchtime. Remember, you haven't eaten for at least 12 hours, so your body is empty and needs refuelling. Another option is porridge, particularly in the winter months; research has shown it helps to offset symptoms of Seasonal Affective Disorder (SAD).

10:30am
Snack

75g(2oz) dried mango, papaya and cranberry mix
Dried fruit contains natural sugars to help keep your blood sugar levels stable.

1:00pm
Lunch

Chicken salad with honey and mustard dressing
One slice pumpernickel bread
150g (pot) low-fat yoghurt

Prepare your own lunch and take it with you to work or on your outings. One of the reasons people find it hard to stick to a healthy food plan is their inability to control what they eat while at work. By preparing your own lunch, you'll know exactly what you're putting into your body.

3:30pm
Snack

2 tbsp reduced-fat hummus
three wheat-free or wholemeal crackers
Hummus contains protein and fibre, so it's not only good for you, but will also put an end to the afternoon slump.

7:30pm
Evening meal

Protein such as fish, chicken or steak, with stir-fried vegetables or a green leaf salad.
A sweet pudding, such as fruit salad or fruit yoghurt, around 30 minutes after your evening meal should satisfy your sweet tooth and stop you craving sweets or chocolates.

The F-word

If you've avoided eating fats because you've been scared of putting on weight, then you may have been doing yourself more harm than good. In fact, fats are an integral part of a healthy, balanced diet.

Fat has always been given bad press. The word alone conjures up negative images: cellulite, obesity and heart problems. But recent research has shown that eating too little fat may mean that you're putting yourself at risk of the very health problems you've been trying to avoid. However, this is not an excuse to overdo the crisps and chocolates!

How fats work

Fats fall into two categories – those that are good for you and those that aren't. The type of fats associated with ill-health, such as obesity, heart disease and cancer, are saturated fats. These tend to be solid at room temperature and include butter, lard and fatty cuts of red meat.

The good fats are called unsaturated fats, made up of monosaturates and polyunsaturates. These fats are liquid at room temperature and are mostly found in vegetable sources, particularly vegetable oils, but also in foods such as chicken, fish and nuts. These foods and oils bring many health benefits, as they supply essential fatty acids that cannot be manufactured by the body. Essential fatty acids help maintain cell structure, lock in the skin's moisture and are required in the production of hormone-like substances called prostaglandins, which regulate the menstrual cycle, reproductive system and blood pressure.

If you cut out fats from your diet, your body suffers in several ways. A deficiency of fats can manifest itself in dry or scaly skin, lowered libido, depression or behavioural problems. Too little fat may also make it harder for you to lose weight.

The different types of fats
Omega-3 and omega-6

It may sound more like a video game than a supplement, but omega-3 is vital for boosting your mood. It is an essential fatty acid found in fish such as salmon, herring, sardines and tuna.

Omega-3 fatty acids are a form of polyunsaturated fats, one of four basic types of fat that the body derives from food. (Cholesterol, saturated fat and monounsaturated fat are the others.) Eating too many foods rich in saturated fats has been associated with the development of degenerative diseases, including heart disease and even cancer. Polyunsaturated fats, on the other hand, are actually good for you. Omega-6s are another type of polyunsaturated fatty acids found in grains, most plant-based oils, poultry, and eggs.

Omega-3s and omega-6s are termed essential fatty acids (EFAs) because they are critical for good health, but the body cannot make them itself. For this reason, they must be obtained from food, thus making outside sources of these fats 'essential'. Key omega-3 fatty acids include eicosapentaenoic acid (EPA) and docosahexanoic acid (DHA), both found primarily in oily cold-water fish. Aside from fresh seaweed, plant foods rarely contain EPA or DHA.

An important omega-6, alpha-linolenic acid (ALA), is found primarily in dark green leafy vegetables, flaxseed oils, and certain vegetable oils. Although eating these affects the body in different ways to EPAs or DHAs, your body's enzymes are able to convert ALA to EPA. All three are important to human health.

How EFAs make you happy

The brain is 60 per cent fat and it needs omega-3s to function efficiently. Researchers have discovered a link between mood disorders and low concentrations of omega-3 fatty acids in the body.

A recent nine-month study of bipolar disorder (manic depression) was stopped after only four months because omega-3s were so effective at improving the participants' moods. And another study has shown that eating fish twice a week is associated with a decrease in the risk of suicide. It is believed that omega-3s help regulate mental health problems because they enhance the ability of brain-cell receptors to comprehend mood-related signals from other neurones in the brain. In other words, the omega-3s help to keep the brain's traffic pattern of thoughts, reactions and reflexes running smoothly and efficiently. Further clinical trials are

Happy tip

Concerned about mercury levels in your seafood? Stick to wild pacific salmon, shrimp, haddock and mid-Atlantic blue crab. Even pregnant women can eat up to 350g (12oz) of these a week without fear of high mercury levels. Always check with your GP if you are concerned about your diet.

Happy tip

Pregnant women and infants need plenty of omega-3s to nourish the developing brain of the foetus and young child. If a pregnant woman gets too few omega-3s, the growing foetus will take what is available from its mother's body. This could set the stage for depression in the mother during pregnancy and after the birth.

underway to investigate whether supplementing the diet with omega-3s will reduce the severity of such psychiatric problems as mild to moderate depression, dementia, bipolar disorder and schizophrenia. Interestingly, the oil used to help the child with a degenerative nerve disorder in the popular film *Lorenzo's Oil* was an omega-3 fatty acid.

How much should I take?

There is no established recommended daily intake for omega-3s, but a healthy diet containing significant amounts of foods rich in this essential fatty acid is clearly sensible. By increasing your intake of omega-3 fatty acids, you will bring the ratio of omega-3 and omega-6 fatty acids back into a healthier, 2-1 or (optimally) 1-1 balance. Too much omega-6 may exacerbate feelings of depression. While it's good to include omega-6 in your diet for a well-balanced eating plan, make sure it doesn't outweigh the amount of mood-boosting omega-3s. Try to reduce your consumption of omega-6-rich foods at the same time that you increase your intake of omega-3-rich foods in the following categories:

Omega-3 rich foods

Oily fish
If you aren't vegetarian, oily fish is the best way to get your omega-3 fats. Nutrition experts recommend one to three oily fish meals a week.

Linseeds
Also known as flax, linseeds are one of the best vegetable sources of omega-3 fats, particularly the essential fat alpha-linolenic acid.

Green leafy vegetables, soya beans, rapeseed oil and walnuts
These also contain omega-3 oils in small quantities.

Pumpkin, sunflower and sesame seeds
These are rich sources of the omega-6 essential fat, alpha-linolenic acid. They're also rich in zinc, iron and other minerals.

Avocados
Termed the 'complete' food by nutritionists, avocados are packed with healthy monounsaturated fats and are also a great source of vitamin E.

Your happiness checklist

Are you?	Possible cause
Fuzzy-headed?	Have you drunk enough water today?
Tearful?	Was your last meal more than three hours ago?
Drowsy, even after eight hours' sleep?	Try some oatcakes with Swiss cheese for a quick pick-me up.
Grumpy and irritable?	Have you been taking your B complex vitamins? If not start now!
Lethargic	Tap your breastbone 50 times with your finger. Open your mouth and say 'ahhh' while you do this.

The GI diet

The GI diet, or glycaemic index diet, is an easy-to-follow, balanced way of eating healthily and losing weight. The following section outlines how your GI system works, and provides a straightforward eating plan. Plus there's a shopping guide, so you won't accidentally slip those biscuits into your trolley!

What is my GI?

When the GI diet first came out, people thought it was an army-based diet – the sort of meals you'd eat if you were a soldier on patrol! But slowly, the GI way of eating has caught on, and now everyone from actress Kim Cattrall to Bill Clinton swear by its energy-boosting and streamlining powers. Even supermarkets have taken to listing GI levels on packaging.

The glycaemic index is a system for measuring the speed at which the digestive system breaks down various foods into glucose, the body's source of energy. Foods are given a rating number, of which glucose is the highest at 100, and all other foods are measured against this. For example, cornflakes, which are digested quickly, have a GI of 77, but porridge has a GI rating of 42, as it's digested more slowly.

All foods fall into one of three groups: carbohydrates, proteins or fats. Only the GI of the carbohydrate element can be measured. Although the index is based on carbohydrates, it's also influenced by protein and fat, both of which act as brakes on the digestive system. (Most carbohydrate-based foods also contain both fat and protein.) For instance, oatmeal is a good source of oils, while red kidney beans supply carbohydrate as well as being a good source of protein. When you eat a meal, it's advisable to combine all three food groups.

The most important principle for maximizing energy levels is to eat mainly foods that are lowest on the GI chart (see opposite) and restrict or avoid foods that score high on the chart. High-GI foods have been shown to increase appetite, which leads to an endless cycle of craving more carbohydrate foods. The GI diet is a sensible, balanced way of eating, which encourages the production of the feel-good chemical serotonin and can help reduce hunger pangs and increase energy levels.

Low GI	Middle GI	High GI
100 per cent bran	artichokes	apple sauce with added sugar
All-bran	bananas	bacon
apple sauce (without sugar)	cantaloupe melon	broad beans
apples	cheese (reduced and half-fat)	canned fruit in syrup
apricots	corn	canned fruit salad in syrup
berries (all types)	couscous	canned fruit salad in syrup
buckwheat	cream cheese (light)	ciabatta
cherries	croissants	coconut oil
clementines/mandarins/satsumas	eggs	custard creams
dried or fresh pasta	fruit yoghurt (regular)	dates
egg whites	granary bread	doughnuts
extra lean beef	honeydew melon	gnocchi
grapefruit	ice-cream (low-fat and no	Granola
grapes	added sugar)	hamburgers
ham (lean)	lean lamb	lard
high-fibre bran	lean pork	mayonnaise
kiwi fruit	mangoes	melba toast
lean back bacon	mayonnaise (low fat and light)	minced beef (regular)
nectarines	minced beef (lean)	muesli (with sugars)
oat bran	peanut butter (sugar free)	muffins
olive oil	pineapple	overripe banana
pork tenderloin	pitta bread	pancakes
pumpernickel	pizza	paté
rabbit	potatoes (boiled, new)	processed meals
rapeseed oil	rye bread	prunes
runner beans	salad dressings (light)	stuffing
salad dressing (fat-free)	Shredded wheat	sushi (rice-based)
sashimi	sirloin steak	toffee popcorn
seafood	sour cream (light)	waffles
skinless chicken breast	soy sauce (regular)	watermelon
Special K cereal	sweet potatoes	white breads
sugar-free muesli	turkey bacon	
Sultana bran	Weetabix	
tofu	wholemeal bread	
turkey breast or leg (skinless)	wild rice	

The GI energy rule

It's 3pm and you're clock-watching. Do you do what most of us do? Make a cup of tea or coffee and maybe have a sneaky chocolate bar? Doing this is extremely bad for your energy levels. Here's why:

A sweet cup of tea with two sugar biscuits may taste great but as soon as these foods hit your bloodstream, you will immediately get the short-term good feeling of a sugar high (called hyperglycaemia). This is when insulin kicks in, drains the excess sugar from the bloodstream to store as fat around your waist and hips, and leaves you with a sugar low (called hypoglycaemia). Because you feel tired again, you probably have just one more biscuit... can you see how the cycle is never-ending?

The GI routine

- Eat three main meals a day: breakfast, lunch and dinner.
- Eat three snacks a day: mid-morning, mid-afternoon and just before bed.
- Never miss a meal or snack. If you do, you may end up craving the wrong foods to give you that 'lift'.
- Breakfast should contain low-GI carbohydrates and low-fat protein.
- Porridge is an ideal way to start the day as it's very low in GI. Add low-fat natural yoghurt or berries for added sweetness.
- For lunch and supper, divide your plate mentally into three sections. One third should contain at least two vegetables; one-third high-GI carbs, such as potato, brown rice or pasta; and the other third meat or seafood. If you are vegetarian, use this last third for tofu, eggs or beans. If you have room, eat a raw salad – this aids digestion.

Carbohydrates

Carbohydrates are the body's main source of calories, and nutritionists recommend that a healthy diet should contain 50 per cent carbohydrates. Recently, carbs have been given a bad reputation, but we need fresh fruit and vegetables to stay healthy and happy.

The digestive system converts carbs into glucose, which dissolves into the bloodstream and is transported to those parts of the body that need energy, such as the muscles and the brain. It's the *type* of carbohydrates you eat that affect your GI level and ultimately your mood (see table on page 73).

Happy tip

The GI diet doesn't restrict you to choosing from just the one column.
Eat a high-GI food, such as yummy toasted ciabatta bread, and spread it with low-GI hummus, lettuce, a squeeze of lemon and a sprinkling of pepper. The low-GI balances the high-GI to give you a medium-GI meal.

Suggested plate listing

Meat or seafood (protein) section
Two eggs
One grilled chicken breast
Salmon, tuna and king prawn sashimi
Lean-beef meatballs (four small)
Mixed pulses

High-GI carb section
Two to three boiled new potatoes
Basmati rice
Wholewheat penne pasta
Spaghetti in fresh tomato sauce

Vegetable section
Boiled or steamed sugar-snap peas
Tomato, basil and olive salad
Wilted spinach
Lettuce and cucumber salad
Pak choi
Runner beans
Steamed broccoli
Lightly steamed courgettes

Smiley GI snacks
Choose snacks that have a low GI-rating to ensure energy levels remain stable. If possible, add a little fat and protein for a balanced mini-meal.

Three oatmeal biscuits
Two rich tea biscuits
One piece of fruit, such as an apple,
Orange, banana, pear, peach or grapefruit
Six dried apricots
Handful of cherries or grapes
four plums
Fresh fruit salad
Cappuccino made with skimmed milk
Handful of raw vegetables such as broccoli, cauliflower, celery, carrots
pot of low-fat, sugar-free yoghurt

To drink or not to drink

Try drinking a glass of water before each meal or snack as part of your GI routine. This will help you feel full, plus it will rehydrate you. Dehydration is one of the biggest causes of low moods.

● Skimmed milk is the best choice to add to tea or porridge.
● Coffee stimulates the production of insulin, which reduces blood sugar levels and then increases appetite. Have just one cup per day and avoid drinking it on an empty stomach (such as first thing in the morning).
● Fruit drinks are high in sugar, even those that are labelled 'no added sugar'. They'll give you a quick boost, but you'll feel worse afterwards. Fruit juices have a lower-GI rating. It's better to eat an actual piece of fruit. Or start your day with a freshly made vegetable juice.
● Alcohol is a no-no, as it has a high-GI rating. Alcohol metabolizes quickly, so it creates a short-term sugar high, which makes you feel great. This is followed by a sugar low, where you're tempted to have another drink to push the sugars up again.

Sugar studies

A recent study gave two groups of people 200 calories of sugar to eat before letting them loose two hours later on a banquet at which they could eat as much as they wanted. On average one of the groups ate 476 calories less than the other group at the feast. What was the difference? The sugar that was given to the group who ate fewer calories was fructose (fruit sugar), which has a very low GI of 22, while the other group was given glucose, which has a GI of 100. This probably explains why a couple of hours after eating a filling Chinese meal it is often the case that people complain that they are hungry – rice and noodles have a relatively high-GI.

Other studies have backed up these findings. In one such study, obese teenage boys were given one of three breakfasts – a high-GI meal of instant oatmeal, a medium-GI meal of whole oats, or a low-GI meal of a vegetable omelette and fruit. Later in the day the voluntary calorie intake after the high-GI meal was 53 per cent greater than it was for the medium-GI meal, and 81 per cent higher than for the low-GI meal.

Supplements

Supplementing your diet is an ideal way to ensure your body is receiving its recommended daily allowance of vitamins and nutrients. The following pages will help you to decide which, if any, supplements you need to boost your mood, energy levels and wellbeing.

Supplements and mood

Before you think that taking a vitamin can cure you of your blues, take some time to consider what *supplement* actually means: something that should be taken in conjunction with a healthy, balanced diet, not *instead* of. The reality is, however, that with our busy, stressful lives, it's extremely difficult to achieve optimum health through diet alone. Plus, recent research has shown that today's fruit and vegetables just don't have as many nutrients and vitamins as they did around 10 years ago, because of the way they are processed, packaged and transported, unlike in the days whenmost people bought locally grown fruit and vegetables daily. So even though you think you're eating a well-balanced, nutritious diet, you may still not be getting all your need from your food.

Eating an organic, primarily fruit and vegetable, diet may be your aim, but life gets in the way. This is where supplements come in. Generally, a good daily multivitamin is enough to ensure that you're getting all the vitamins and minerals your body needs. If your moods have taken a turn for the worse or you're on a rollercoaster of energy and mood swings, supplements can help to get the balance back.

Feeling happy is not just a matter of including serotonin- and norepinephrine-producing foods in your eating plan. There are also important links between vitamins, minerals and depression. Certain vitamin and mineral deficiencies may aggravate depression. In addition, if you are depressed and not eating properly, your body may become deficient in various nutrients, setting up a vicious circle that can be difficult to break. Certain situations make you more prone to develop a nutrient deficiency, such as a recent illness, stress, over-exercising, a change in routine, or lack of (or broken) sleep cycles. The quiz on the next page will help you assess whether you are deficient in any important vitamins or minerals.

Quick supplement assessment quiz

The reason you have been feeling low and lethargic may be quite simple –
you may be lacking one or more of the key vitamins and minerals in your
diet. First see if any of the descriptions below ring true.

● You haven't been eating properly, either as a result of working too hard
  or because generally you've not felt like eating.
● You've been feeling unwell or just 'not yourself'.
● You take prescription drugs, whether as regular medication or a short
  course of antibiotics.
● You feel stressed.
● You've stripped your body of much-needed nutrients due to over-
  consumption of alcohol, tea and coffee.
● You've had a particularly heavy menstrual period.

If two or more of these statements apply to you, you should see your GP.
Your doctor can arrange for some simple tests to discover whether you are
deficient in the B vitamins or vitamin C. If you are deficient, it's likely that
you have had low levels for several months. These vitamins are the most
common deficiencies in people experiencing low moods, usually due to
the effects of stress, poor diet and lack of exercise.

   If you wish to embark on a supplement programme, the following
guide will help you see which particular supplement is the most effective
for you.

A–Z of supplements

Vitamin A/Betacarotene

What it does Strengthens your immune system and is needed for healthy skin function. If you suffer from urinary tract infections, you may need to increase your intake of Vitamin A. Also necessary for normal eye vision: keep your intake high if you do a lot of computer work and suffer from eye strain.

How do I know if I'm deficient? If you're continually getting colds, suffer from diarrhoea or have blurred vision, you may be advised to increase your intake of Vitamin A. It is quite rare for adults to be deficient in this vitamin.

How much should I take? 5,000IU per day, or, if you're taking a betacarotene supplement (this is converted to vitamin A in the body), take 10–30mg. If you smoke, check with your doctor before taking vitamin A.

What foods is it in? Spinach, apricots, broccoli, carrots, pumpkin, sweet potato, asparagus, melon, kale, liver

B vitamins

The B group of vitamins help energize brain cells and manufacture important chemicals to keep your moods high. Vitamin B6, for example, plays a major role in the making of serotonin. Too little, and you'll walk around feeling down in the dumps. What's more, B-complex vitamins enhance communication between brain cells so that other important brain chemicals can work together to keep things running smoothly.

Vitamin B1 (Thiamine)

What it does Thiamine, or vitamin B1, helps build and maintain healthy brain cells. It's essential for energy production and digestion. It also helps the body utilize protein correctly.

How do I know if I'm deficient? Eye pains, irritability, poor concentration, poor memory, stomach pains, tingling hands, rapid or erratic heartbeat.

How much should I take? 25–100mg per day

What foods is it in? Watercress, squash, courgettes, lamb, peppers, asparagus, mushrooms, peas, lettuce, cauliflower, cabbage, tomatoes, Brussels sprouts, beans

Happy tip If you're on the contraceptive pill, an antibiotic course, or drink more than three cups of tea and coffee each day, you should stock up on vitamin B1 foods. If you take it as a supplement form, take the B complex with your morning breakfast.

Vitamin B2 (Riboflavin)

What it does Vitamin B2 is essential for growth and the functioning of body tissue. A deficiency can cause symptoms of depression. People at risk include women who take oral contraceptives and those in the second trimester of pregnancy.

How do I know if I'm deficient? Sensitivity to bright lights, eczema or dermatitis, cracked lips, sore tongue, dull or oily hair.

How much should I take? 25–100mg per day

What foods is it in? Mushrooms, watercress, cabbage, asparagus, broccoli, pumpkin, mackerel, milk, bamboo shoots, tomatoes, wheatgerm

Happy tip Take selenium alongside vitamin B2 to improve the efficiency of the latter.

Vitamin B3 (niacin)

What it does Vitamin B3, or niacin, is essential to help lift your mood. It is needed for energy production and to help you think clearly. It's also good for problematic skin. If your blood sugar levels are constantly unbalanced, vitamin B3 will help sort them out.

How do I know if I'm deficient? A deficiency of this vitamin can cause depression. Left untreated, it can lead to psychosis and dementia. Symptoms of a vitamin B3 deficiency include agitation, anxiety, and mental lethargy.

How much should I take? 500mg twice daily

What foods is it in? Mushrooms, tuna, chicken, salmon, asparagus, cabbage, lamb, mackerel, turkey, tomatoes, courgettes, squash, cauliflower, wholewheat breads and pasta

Happy tip If you're on antibiotics, make sure you are getting enough niacin, as these medicines can rob your body of this essential vitamin.

Vitamin B5 (pantothenic acid)

What it does Boosts your metabolism and soothes frazzled nerves because of its ability to counteract the negative effects of stress.

How do I know if I'm deficient? You may feel apathetic, have difficulty concentrating, have burning feet or tender heels, lack of energy or feel anxious and tense.

How much should I take? 300mg per day. Best taken within a B-complex vitamin.

What foods is it in? Mushrooms, watercress, broccoli, alfalfa sprouts, peas, lentils, tomatoes, cabbage, celery, strawberries, eggs, squash, avocados, wholewheat

Happy tip If you're feeling stressed, up your intake of foods rich in vitamin B5, as this vitamin helps to make the acetylcholine neurotransmitter, which regulates your response to stressful situations.

Vitamin B6 (pyridoxine)

What it does Helps to convert tryptophan into serotonin. Helps balance sex hormones, very useful for sufferers of PMT. If you are on the contraceptive pill, you should supplement your diet with vitamin B6, as the pill robs the body of this vitamin.

How do I know if I'm deficient? Irritability, depression or nervousness, muscle tremors or cramps, lack of energy, tingling hands, water retention, flaky skin.

How much should I take? 50mg twice a day for two weeks, between meals. Then 50mg once daily for three weeks, between meals. Thereafter, take a good B-complex formula or a multivitamin and mineral supplement to maintain healthy levels of this vitamin.

What foods is it in? Chicken, pork, liver, kidney, fish, nuts and legumes, watercress, cauliflower, cabbage, peppers, bananas, squash, broccoli, asparagus, red kidney beans, onions, Brussels sprouts

Happy tip Take alongside zinc and magnesium, first thing in the morning with your breakfast.

Vitamin B12 (cyanocobalamin)

What it does Vitamin B12 helps the blood carry oxygen around the body, so it's a must for creating and sustaining energy levels. Vitamin B12 also helps make the myelin sheath, the fatty layer that insulates and protects the nerves. A lack of vitamin B12 means that the nerves aren't as thickly coated, so you may overeact to certain situations. This could mean the difference between being slightly annoyed that you spilt your coffee and bursting into tears at the injustice of the world. If you smoke (don't!), this vitamin helps to offset the negative health effects your habit brings.

How do I know if I'm deficient? Recent studies have shown that there is a definite benefit to be gained by giving vitamin B12 to patients suffering from depression, fatigue and mental illnesses of other kinds. Even a slight deficiency of B12 is found to produce marked symptoms such as a lack of energy, constipation, irritability, anxiety, tenseness, eczema or dermatitis, and your mouth maybe over-sensitive to hot or cold foods.

How much should I take? 300–500 micrograms (mcg) twice a day

What foods is it in? Oysters, sardines, tuna, lamb, eggs, shrimps, cottage cheese, turkey and chicken, cheese.

Happy tip If you've had a late night or are going through a stressful time your body won't be able to react calmly or clearly to certain situations. Help cushion your frazzled nerves by starting the day with a glass of freshly squeezed orange juice or a banana.

Vitamin C

What it does Most of us know that Vitamin C is the wunderkind when it comes to beating colds and flu. But this vitamin does much more than keep sniffles at bay. Vitamin C helps the body manufacture dopamine, known as the brain's pleasure chemical. Dopamine is an important neurotransmitter in the central nervous system, regulating movements, emotions, motivation and feelings of pleasure. Vitamin C is also necessary to help turn food into energy, plus it fights antioxidants, caused by pollution, smoking and processed foods.

How do I know if I'm deficient? A lack of vitamin C is the easiest vitamin deficiency to spot. You'll suffer colds frequently, have a noticeable lack of energy, bleeding or sore gums, and you may notice that you bruise easily.

How much should I take? 1,000–10,000mg per day

What foods is it in? Peppers, watercress, cabbage, broccoli, cauliflower, strawberries, lemons, kiwi fruit, peas, melons, oranges, limes, tomatoes

Happy tip Keep a watch on your bowel movements. If your stools are not firm, then your vitamin C dosage may be too high and be causing acidity in your stomach. Lower your dosage until your stools return to firmness.

Vitamin E

What it does Most people use creams containing Vitamin E, and it's true that it's especially good at keeping your skin clear and youthful. It also helps the body use oxygen, thus increasing your energy levels.

How do I know if I'm deficient? You may experience a lack of desire for sex, exhaustion after light exercise, bruise easily, varicose veins, have infertility problems.

How much should I take? 1,000mg per day

What foods is it in? Sunflower seeds, peanuts, sesame seeds, peas, tuna, sardines, wheatgerm, salmon, sweet potatoes, almonds

Happy tip If you eat an especially fatty diet, vitamin E will help counteract the negative effects. Also recommended if you are on the contraceptive pill.

Potassium

What it does Potassium is especially important if you tire easily, or suffer from afternoon tiredness, as it helps to control your blood sugar levels. It's also ideal for supporting your nervous system. A potassium deficiency can occur after a bout of diarrhoea or illness.

How do I know if I'm deficient? Pins and needles, irritability, nausea, swollen abdomen, low blood pressure, mental apathy.

How much should I take? 200–3,500mg per day

What foods is it in? Cabbage, celery, courgettes, radishes, cauliflower, mushrooms, pumpkin, molasses

Happy tip Take alongside magnesium, as this helps the potassium to function more efficiently.

Folate

What it does Folate is another B vitamin that has been linked to depression and poor moods. It is the naturally occurring form of folic acid. Low moods are considered the most common symptom of a folate deficiency.

How do I know if I'm deficient? Lack of energy, feeling down or blue, feeling anxious and tense, little or no appetite.

How much should I take? 400–1,000mcg per day

What foods is it in? Spinach, peanuts, sprouts, asparagus, sesame seeds, hazelnuts, broccoli, cashew nuts, cauliflower, walnuts, avocados, wheatgerm

Happy tip Make sure that your B-complex supplement contains folate or folic acid to get all your vitamins in one tablet.

Zinc

What it does Zinc is an extremely important mineral, as it controls hormones from your ovaries. Thus a deficiency can lead to more severe PMT. Zinc helps your body cope with stress effectively and is essential for maintaining consistent energy levels. It also helps to keep the senses sharp, and encourages a healthy immune system. It is critical for proper growth and development in children.

How do I know if I'm deficient? White marks on your fingernails, lacklustre skin, feeling down and generally unhappy, lack of appetite.

How much should I take? 15–50mg per day

What foods is it in? Red meat, oysters, ginger root, lamb, pecan nuts, haddock, green peas, dry split peas, sunflower seeds, shrimps, turnips, brazil nuts, egg yolk, wholewheat grain, rye, oats, peanuts, almonds

Happy tip If you have an excessively high sugar intake, make sure you include zinc in your diet plan, to counteract sugar come-downs.

Calcium

What it does A study of 500 PMT-prone women found that when they took 1,200mg supplements of calcium daily their mood swings, depression and irritability eased by 50 per cent. Calcium helps the nervous system receive and process messages from the brain, helping to maintain a balanced and calm mind. Calcium also helps to regulate hormones. Your body suppresses the bad-mood hormones if your calcium supplies are adequate, but releases these hormones if you're not getting enough calcium. Women who suffer from PMT appear to have elevated levels of these hormones during their menstrual cycle, and this explains why the symptoms of PMT, such as cramping, irritability, and depression, are similar to those of a calcium-deficient state.

How do I know if I'm deficient? You may suffer from insomnia, nervousness, joint pain, muscle cramps, and more severe PMT symptoms.

How much should I take? 800–1,200mg per day

What foods is it in? Cheddar cheese, Swiss cheese, almonds, brewer's yeast, parsley, globe artichokes, prunes, pumpkin seeds, cooked dried beans, cabbage, turnips

Happy tip If you're particularly stressed or have a stressful time coming up, make sure you're eating a calcium-rich diet to offset the negative physical and emotional effects that stress causes.

Magnesium

What it does If you're feeling wound up, then your body is going to mirror your emotions. By including magnesium in your diet you'll encourage healthy muscles to relax and help soothe period cramps. Several British studies have found that taking 200mg of magnesium per day helped relieve water retention and mood swings in women. Magnesium and vitamin B6 are needed for the body to produce serotonin. When depression or a panic disorder are persistent – and especially when the usual drugs have limited effect – supplementing with magnesium and vitamin B6 may provide significant relief. It may take six weeks or more of treatment for the effects to be felt.

How do I know if I'm deficient? You may find it difficult to sleep at night, experience feelings of nervousness or anxiety, have constipation, lack of appetite or feel lethargic or depressed.

How much should I take? 400–800mg per day

What foods is it in? Almonds, cashew nuts, brewer's yeast, brazil nuts, peanuts, pecan nuts, cooked beans, garlic, raisins, green peas, potato skin, crab

Happy tip Taking calcium along with magnesium may lessen an over-reaction to stress that some research has linked to anxiety and panic attacks.

Inositol

What it does Inositol is a B vitamin required for the activity of several important neurotransmitters, including serotonin. Depressed people often have low levels of inositol. In one clinical study, subjects were given 1 gram of inositol per day. The results showed that they had therapeutic results similar to those of common antidepressant drugs, but with no unwanted side-effects.

How do I know if I'm deficient? If you've been especially grumpy or feeling nervous, you may be deficient in inositol.

How much should I take? 500mg three times a day for one week. After one week, if there is no improvement, discontinue use. Otherwise continue taking 500mg three times a day as and when needed.

What foods is it in? Lecithin granules, pulses, soya flour, eggs, fish, liver, citrus fruits, melon, nuts, wheatgerm, brewer's yeast

Happy tip If you've suffered from a bout of diarrhoea or take the contraceptive pill, you may need to supplement your diet with inositol.

Chromium

What it does Helps to balance blood sugar levels, reduce cravings.

How do I know if I'm deficient? If you feel irritable or dizzy after six hours without food (as opposed to merely hungry) or when waking in the morning, you may be deficient in chromium.

How much should I take? 20–200mcg per day

What foods is it in? Brewer's yeast, wholemeal bread, rye bread, potatoes, wheatgerm, green peppers, chicken, apples, butter, parsnips, cornmeal, lamb, Swiss cheese

Happy tip If you eat a lot of white bread (naughty!), then chromium will help rebalance those sugar lows.

Selenium

What it does Selenium is an antioxidant that helps protect the immune system against pollution, stress, cigarette smoke and the free radicals released from fried foods. It has a mood-elevating effect when taken in regions where food supply is deficient in selenium. It also assists the effectiveness of vitamin E in the body. Selenium is good for strengthening the immune system, which may become impaired from stress.

How do I know if I'm deficient? Signs of premature ageing, constant colds and/or infections.

How much should I take? 25–100mcg per day

What foods is it in? Tuna, oysters, mushrooms, herrings, cottage cheese, cabbage, beef liver, courgettes, cod, chicken

Happy tip Take alongside a daily multivitamin which contains vitamins A, C and E.

Iron

What it does Iron is essential for the production of energy. It transports oxygen and carbon dioxide to and from cells.

How do I know if I'm deficient? You may feel listless, have anaemia, a sore tongue and feel fatigued.

How much should I take? 15–25mg per day

What foods is it in? Pumpkin seeds, parsley, almonds, prunes, cashew nuts, raisins, brazil nuts, walnuts, dates, pork, sesame seeds, pecan nuts

Happy tip Take iron alongside a vitamin C supplement as vitamin C actually increases the absorption of iron by the body.

Other types of supplement
St John's wort (hypericum)

St John's wort, sometimes called the 'sunshine herb', is a bushy perennial plant with numerous star-shaped yellow flowers. Native to many parts of the world, including Europe and the United States, it has been used as a herbal remedy for about 2000 years. St John's wort is commonly available in dried herb, liquid extract, tincture extract and tablet form.

Historically used to repair nerve damage, St John's wort is now becoming more widely used (and recommended by some doctors) to help ease depression. Numerous studies have researched the positive effects of St John's wort on people with mild to moderate depression. In nearly all cases, St John's wort has proved to be almost, if not as, effective as prescribed antidepressants in elevating moods. In August 1996, the *British Medical Journal* published an overview and analysis of randomized clinical trials, which reviewed studies to date into the link between St John's wort and depression. The report concluded that, '*There is evidence that extracts of hypericum are more effective than placebo for the treatment of mild to moderately severe depressive disorders*.'

How does it work?

No one is quite sure how St John's wort helps fight depression, but research indicates that it is the hypericin, a natural substance found in the yellow flowers, which is the key ingredient (among the 50 active ingredients found in the plant). The hypericin works in a similar way to SSRIs, or Selective Serotonin Re-uptake Inhibitors, such as Prozac (fluoxetine). Many medical professionals believe that depression may be caused by an imbalance of serotonin. SSRIs help to correct this imbalance of serotonin activity by stopping reabsorption of the serotonin and effectively recycling it (see pages 13, 14 for more on SSRIs).

Cautions

Some users of St John's wort experience fatigue, restlessness and extreme sensitivity to light. You should not use St John's wort if you are:
● Severely depressed; the herb only seems to have a positive effect on mild to moderate depression. If you are severely depressed, always

Happy tip

Migraine headaches have been linked to low serotonin levels. Studies are ongoing to determine if 5-HTP, which may boost the brain's serotonin levels, can help to reduce the intensity, frequency and duration of this extremely painful type of headache. Start by taking 50mg three times a day, but do not exceed 100mg three times a day.

seek the advice of your GP. **NB** You shouldn't stop taking prescription medicine in order to take St John's wort (or start using it if you're already taking prescription medicine) without talking to your GP first;

- Already using antidepressants like Prozac or lithium;
- Photosensitive (extremely sensitive to sunlight);
- Pregnant or breast-feeding;
- Taking the contraceptive pill, as it's thought St John's wort can make the pill less effective;
- Taking blood-thinning medication (anti-coagulants) such as warfarin, as St John's wort can undermine the effect of the anti-coagulant.

There is often a difference in the quality, potency and purity between each brand on the market, meaning it can be hard to evaluate its effectiveness. Remember to check the packaging of the particular product you buy for usage instructions.

Some medical professionals believe that St John's wort should be made a prescription-only drug, as is now the case in Ireland. The herb was widely available in Ireland until early January 2000, when the Irish Medicines Board ordered it to be removed from shop shelves with the argument that any product on the market that makes medicinal claims requires authorization.

How quickly does it work?

You should start to feel an improvement after about six weeks and before three months. If you don't, find out if there are alternative options.

SAMe

SAMe (pronounced 'sammy') is short for S-adenosylmethionine, a molecule produced continually by the body to fuel numerous vital functions. Discovered in 1952, the popularity of SAMe has soared recently with talk of its ability to ease depression as effectively as the more well-known prescription antidepressants. (Proponents say SAMe also works faster than antidepressants and with virtually no side-effects.)

Long prescribed by European doctors for both arthritis and depression, SAMe recently became available in the United States as an over-the-counter supplement. It is also emerging as an effective therapy for arthritis, fibromyalgia, certain liver disorders, and possibly even Alzheimer's disease. In the UK, SAMe is only currently available on prescription.

How does it work?

The body manufactures SAMe from methionine, an amino acid found in protein-rich foods, and adenosine triphosphate (ATP), an energy-producing compound found in all the body's cells. The SAMe molecule then donates a piece of itself (a methyl group) to body tissues and organs, providing a critical link in the process of methylation, a chemical reaction that occurs billions of times a second throughout the body. In giving up a part of itself, SAMe promotes cell growth and repair.

SAMe also contributes to the formation of key compounds in the brain, including the neurotransmitter dopamine and the mood-enhancer serotonin. In addition, it helps to maintain desirable levels of glutathione, a major antioxidant that protects against cell damage from oxygen molecules called free radicals. Taken as a supplement, SAMe compensates for any deficiencies and encourages the body to run efficiently.

Several studies indicate that SAMe eases mild to moderately severe depression. Clinical trials have concluded that it appears to work as well as the frequently prescribed tricyclic antidepressants. Just as importantly, it works faster, often starting to improve mood within a week. This contrasts significantly with standard antidepressants, where the effects can take several weeks to become apparent. In a University of California study of 17 severely depressed adults, 62 per cent of the participants who took SAMe for four weeks (1,600mg daily) showed significant improvements in symptoms, compared to 50 per cent of those who used desipramine (a conventional antidepressant). Unlike many prescription antidepressants, which often cause unpleasant side-effects such as drowsiness, dry mouth and constipation, SAMe appears to cause few, if any, side-effects.

How to take it

● Look for enteric-coated SAMe; it's more readily absorbed by the body in this form and remains chemically stable for much longer (the coating protects it from exposure to air).

- To avoid a toxic build up of homocysteine molecules (which are formed when SAMe breaks down), take a high-quality vitamin B-complex supplement alongside the SAMe. These vitamins disarm homocysteine, which in high concentrations poses the risk of various health problems including heart attack and stroke. A standard recommendation is to take 100mg of a B complex once a day, regardless of the SAMe dose.
- If you're particularly sensitive to medications, start out with half the recommended daily dosage and work up to the full amount after a week.
- For depression, arthritis, fibromylagia and liver disorders, take 400mg of SAMe twice a day. If symptoms fail to improve after three weeks, try increasing your dose to 400mg three times a day. On the other hand, if symptoms lessen when you're taking 400mg twice a day, you can try to lower the dose to 200mg.
- SAMe is best absorbed on an empty stomach, so try to take it about one hour before or two hours after meals. If nausea or heartburn develop, take it with plenty of water.
- To prevent insomnia, avoid taking SAMe late in the day. Most people report a mild energy boost with the supplement.
- SAMe can safely be combined with other natural antidepressants such as St John's wort, as well as conventional antidepressants.

Cautions

In rare cases, daily doses of 400mg or higher may cause mild stomach upset, dry mouth, and insomnia. At extremely high doses, the supplement may cause diarrhoea and heartburn.

- If you suffer from severe depression, don't take SAMe without consulting your doctor first. This precaution is particularly important if you have a bipolar disorder, because SAMe could trigger or exacerbate mania in such cases.
- If you're taking prescription antidepressants, don't discontinue them or reduce your dosage without consulting your doctor.
- SAMe should lift depression relatively quickly. If you don't notice a significant improvement after four weeks, see your doctor. You may need a different category of antidepressant.

5-HTP

The nutrient 5-HTP, otherwise known as 5-hydroxytryptophan, is a derivative of the amino acid tryptophan. A mood-enhancing chemical, 5-HTP has attracted attention because of its ability to increase pain tolerance, induce sleep and affect how hunger is perceived. Unlike many other supplements (and drugs), which have molecules too large to pass from the bloodstream into the brain, 5-HTP has small molecules that have no difficulty passing through. Once in the brain, they're converted into serotonin.

How does it work?

The body produces its own supply of 5-HTP from tryptophan, found in high-protein foods such as chicken, fish, beef, and dairy products. Any healthy diet should include tryptophan-rich sources such as these. However, due to our varied (and not always balanced) diets, it is sometimes necessary to take 5-HTP in supplement form. This supplement is extracted from the seeds of the African plant, *Griffonia simplicifolia*.

Research shows that 5-HTP has many benefits, the primary one being its significant role in lifting mood and alleviating depression. 5-HTP does this by increasing the brain's serotonin levels. A number of European studies offer examples of people with depression who found little relief from traditional antidepressant drugs, yet obtained good results with 5-HTP.

If you suffer from insomnia, it's worth talking to your GP or nutritionist about 5-HTP. The compound appears to reduce the amount of time it takes to fall asleep, as well as increasing the duration of REM and deep slumber. In some studies, people who took 5-HTP also reported feeling more rested when they woke.

How to take it

5-HTP can be taken in either tablet or capsule form. To help boost moods and alleviate anxiety and panic attacks, take 50–100mg three times a day. It's best to take it on an empty stomach to help absorption. If you are taking 5-HTP to help you sleep, take 100mg 30 minutes before going to bed, after a carbohydrate meal.

Cautions

Many experts consider 5-HTP supplements very safe and effective; adverse reactions to the supplement in a handful of users several years ago were traced to contaminants in the manufacturing process, but the problems appear to have been resolved.

Reduce the dose if drowsiness occurs. Also, because of the risk of drowsiness, avoid driving or performing any potentially dangerous task until you've determined how the supplement (at various dosages) affects you.

- The combination of 5-HTP with conventional antidepressants may cause such unwanted reactions as anxiety, confusion, increased heart rate, excessive perspiration, and diarrhoea.
- Consult your doctor before combining 5-HTP with St John's wort.
- Avoid taking 5-HTP with sedating antihistamines; the combination can lead to drowsiness.
- Don't take 5-HTP with over-the-counter cold remedies or any medications containing ephedrine or pseudoephedrine, because anxiety, confusion, or other serious side-effects may develop.
- Muscle relaxants could cause excessive drowsiness when combined with 5-HTP.
- Drowsiness may develop if 5-HTP is taken with a narcotic pain reliever such as codeine or morphine.
- Consult your doctor before trying 5-HTP if you take levodopa for
- Parkinson's disease, because anxiety, confusion, or other adverse reactions may occur when the two substances are combined.
- Psychiatric medications such as buspirone (to combat anxiety) and lithium (to prevent mania) may combine with 5-HTP in such a way that anxiety, confusion, or other serious side-effects develop.

Side-effects

Side-effects of 5-HTP are typically mild but may include nausea, constipation, wind, drowsiness or a decreased sex drive. Nausea, should it occur, commonly disappears after a few days.

Mood-enhancer checklist

This guide will tell you the source of the vitamins and how they affect your mood.

Vitamin	What it does	Source
Vitamin A/ Betacarotene	Boosts the immune system.	Apricots, asparagus, broccoli, cantaloupe melon, carrots, kale, liver, pumpkin, spinach, sweet potatoes
Vitamin B1 (thiamine)	Helps the body utilise protein.	Beer, brewer's yeast, brown rice, chickpeas, kidney beans, kidney and liver, pork, rice bran, salmon, soya beans, sunflower seeds, wheatgerm, wholegrain products, wheat and rye
Vitamin B2 (riboflavin)	Helps to turn fats, sugars and protein into energy. Good for stabilising moods.	Almonds, brewer's yeast, cheese, chicken, mushrooms, wheatgerm
Vitamin B3 (niacin)	Helps balance blood sugar levels. Essential for energy production.	Beef liver, brewer's yeast, chicken, eggs, fish, sunflower seeds, turkey
Vitamin B5 (pantothenic acid)	Involved in energy production. Essential for nerves. Helps to make anti-stress hormones.	Blue cheese, brewer's yeast, carrots, corn, eggs, lentils, liver, lobster, meats, peanuts, peas, soya beans, sunflower seeds, wheatgerm, wholegrain products
Vitamin B6 (pyridoxine)	Helps balance sex hormones – particularly good for PMT. Natural anti-depressant.	Avocados, bananas, bran, brewer's yeast, carrots, hazelnuts, lentils, rice, salmon, shrimps, soya beans, sunflower seeds, tuna, walnuts, wheatgerm, wholegrain flour
Vitamin B12 (cyanocobalamin) Biotin	Helps the blood carry oxygen – good for energy levels. Essential for nervous system.	Cheese, clams, eggs, fish, meat, milk and milk products

The Happy Plan

Vitamin	What it does	Source
Biotin	Helps maintain healthy nervous system.	Brewer's yeast, brown rice, cashew nuts, cheese, chicken, eggs, lentils, mackerel, meat, milk, oats, peanuts, peas, soya beans, sunflower seeds, tuna, walnuts
Calcium	Promotes healthy nerves, reduces menstrual cramps.	Almonds, brazil nuts, cheese, kelp, milk, molasses, salmon (canned), sardines (canned), shrimp, soya beans, yoghurt
Vitamin C	Strengthens immune system. Helps make the anti-stress hormone and turns food into energy.	Blackcurrants, broccoli, Brussels sprouts, cabbage, grapefruit, green peppers, guava, kale, lemons, oranges, papaya, potatoes, spinach, strawberries, tomatoes, watercress
Folic acid	Essential for brain and nerve function.	Barley, brewer's yeast, chickpeas, fruits, green leafy vegetables, lentils, peas, rice, soya beans, wholewheat, wheatgerm
Magnesium	Good for nervous system, PMT cramps.	Almonds, fish, green leafy vegetables, kelp, molasses, nuts, soya beans, sunflower seeds, wheatgerm
Chromium	Helps to balance blood sugar levels.	Apples, butter, brewer's yeast, chicken, cornmeal, eggs, green peppers, lamb, oysters, parsnips, potatoes, Swiss cheese, wheatgerm, wholemeal bread and rye bread
Iron	Transports oxygen and carbon dioxide to and from cells. Vital for energy production.	Almonds, brazil nuts, cashew nuts, cooked dried beans, dates, parsley, pecan nuts, pork, prunes, pumpkin seeds, raisins, sesame seeds, walnuts

Vitamin	What it does	Source
Manganese	Stabilises blood sugar levels.	Beetroot, blackberries, celery, endive, grapes, lettuce, lima beans, oats, okra, pineapples, raspberries, strawberries, watercress
Potassium	Promotes healthy nerves, helps secretion of insulin for blood sugar to produce constant energy.	Avocado, bananas, cabbage, cauliflower, celery, citrus fruits, courgettes, endive, lentils, milk, molasses, mushrooms, nuts, parsley, parsnips, radishes, raisins, sardines (canned), spinach, watercress
Selenium	Protects the immune system against pollution, stress, cigarette smoke and the free radicals released from fried foods.	Broccoli, cabbage, celery, chicken, egg yolk, garlic, liver, milk, mushrooms, onions, seafood, wheatgerm, whole grains
Zinc	Helps you to cope with stress effectively.	Egg yolk, fish, all meat, milk, molasses, oysters, sesame seeds, soya beans, sunflower seeds, turkey, wheatgerm, wholegrains
Fibre	Helps relieve sluggish bowels and increase energy levels.	Barley, black-eyed beans, brown rice, buckwheat, chickpeas, fresh fruit, fresh vegetables, kidney beans, lentils, oats, rye, wholewheat
Essential fatty acids (EFAs)	Helps relieve depression.	Herring, mackerel, salmon, sardines, tuna; linseeds, pumpkin, sesame and sunflowers seeds and their unprocessed oils
Coenzyme Q10	Boosts immunity, boosts energy levels.	Beef, mackerel, sardines, soya oil, spinach

Part 3
Happy Life

Happy Life

We've looked at your natural body cycle and how the foods you eat might be making you happy, sad, angry, mellow, irritable or calm. This section looks at the way you choose to live your life and how this affects your state of happiness. Exercise, work, relationships, hobbies, home, health, creativity and spirituality can all play an important role.

Making exercise work

The benefits of regular exercise are numerous. Exercise builds muscle, burns fat, makes heart and lungs work more efficiently, lowers the density of damaging sugars in the blood and is a major factor in combating osteoporosis. Best of all, and probably most importantly, exercise makes you look better and feel better, since it releases endorphins, the brain's mood-elevating compounds.

Exercise and mood

Research shows that people who exercise on a regular basis have lower levels of stress than their fellow couch potatoes. Ironically, it's when you most feel like hibernating and snuggling up on the sofa that your body benefits the most from getting in gear and moving about. It doesn't necessarily matter what sort of exercise you do; as long as you get your body moving and your heart rate pumping, your mind and your body will reap the benefits.

Take a brisk country walk and you feel better, right? Even if it's raining, freezing cold or even snowing, you return home feeling invigorated, exhilarated and yes, happy. It's not just that you're happy to be back in the warmth (although this could be part of it!), your happiness vibe has come from the benefits of exercise. It's something almost all of us can do, every day of the year and yet most of us don't. Why? The usual reasons people give for lack of exercise are time constraints, money issues, lack of motivation or lack of knowledge of the type of exercise to do.

So, let's stop right there. All these reasons are simply excuses. If you can walk, you can exercise. It's free, we all learnt to do it when we were about nine months old and it can be done almost anywhere, at any time.

The UK's National Institute of Mental Health estimates that around 30 minutes of physical activity not only helps to lift your mood, but also keeps it elevated for at least 24 hours. Imagine, then, that you do the recommended 30 minutes of exercise every day. Every day your mood will be elevated, so there should be nothing to stop you!

Exercise and depression

The Mental Health Foundation believes that exercise therapy, delivered in an appropriately supervized context, could make a significant difference to many people with mild or moderate depression. Patients may find that using exercise as a treatment for mild or moderate depression has a beneficial therapeutic effect on their moods. Exercise will also help them make sustainable lifestyle changes that will benefit them in the long run. Ultimately, says the MHF, it could reduce the cost burden on the NHS prescription budget, by giving GPs greater freedom to explore non-pharmacological approaches to treatment.

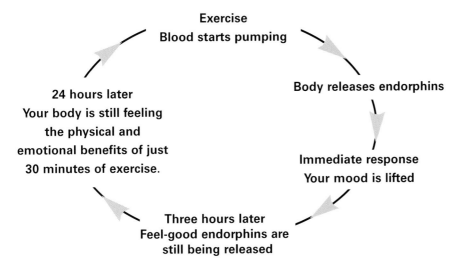

Exercise
Blood starts pumping

Body releases endorphins

Immediate response
Your mood is lifted

Three hours later
Feel-good endorphins are still being released

24 hours later
Your body is still feeling the physical and emotional benefits of just 30 minutes of exercise.

What type of exercise is best for me?

We're not all the same. If you're not motivated by your exercise routine there's no point. The quiz on pages 108–111 will help you find a type of activity that will best suit your personality and lifestyle.

Aerobic exercise

Aerobic exercise is any large muscle activity that you can sustain for two to three minutes or longer. The word aerobic actually means 'with oxygen'. In other words, this form of exercise increases the flow of oxygen to your muscles, and helps dispel any fogginess or negativity in your mind. Choose from walking, gardening, hiking, bicycling, lap swimming, jogging or cross-country skiing. How often should you exercise? Perform any aerobic exercise for 20 to 60 minutes at least five times a week.

Resistance exercise or strength training

Strength training increases muscle strength and mass, bone strength and the body's metabolism. A review published in the *Journal of Ageing and Physical Activity* found that weight training in particular can improve mood. It found that adults who included weight training in their exercise programme were not only happier, but had more overall vigour and calmness. There are various ways to increase your body's strength. These include free weights, weight machines, callisthenics and resistance training. How often should you do it? Do resistance training at least twice a week for 20 minutes at a time.

Isotonic exercise

This particular form of weight training exercise is probably lesser known by its name, although we all tend to perform some type of isotonic exercise in our regime. Isotonic exercise involves contracting your muscles, without moving your joints. For instance, doing sit-ups, throwing a ball or playing tennis.

Stretching

Stretching your body to maintain its flexibility is probably the most underrated part of an exercise programme. While stretching should not constitute the entire workout, it's important to allow the connective tissue surrounding your muscle fibres to lengthen, which in turn allows your body to support more vigorous activity.

Yoga

Yoga, dance, tai chi and Pilates are excellent forms of isotonic exercise that strengthen muscles and should be incorporated into your weekly exercise schedule. You'll find that you not only benefit physically from this, but mentally as well.

How to get your 30 minutes of exercise a day

Can't fit in 30 minutes at once? Researchers now say that it's just as beneficial to do three 10-minute bursts each day. Walk to a sandwich bar 10 minutes from your work. By the time you return to the office you'll already have completed 20 minutes. Even parking further away from the supermarket when you go shopping will add to your daily allowance. Be inventive with your time – it doesn't matter how or where you exercise, just as long as you do it. If you have a busy life, don't expect exercise slots just to pop up in your diary. Part of the secret of getting more exercise into you life is to schedule activity sessions in advance. Try to write exercise sessions in your diary, or on the calendar, just as you would appointments, meetings or other events.

Case Study

Bea Thompson, 43, had been suffering from anxiety and depression for several years before being referred to the Active Lifestyles Exercise Referral Scheme in Bromley.

At my low point, around October 2002, I was very ill and debilitated. I'm a graduate and I've worked in business and management, but I was homeless and had been socially housed in a completely different area. For about a year, I might have had interaction once a week – my mammoth task was to go out and make sure I had enough benefits or electricity, or to see a doctor.

In the middle of 2003 I saw a leaflet for the Active Lifestyles scheme in the GP surgery. I asked my doctor if he would refer me, as I had a feeling that exercise would be good for me. However, I felt very anxious about going into the gym environment. The night before I couldn't sleep because I was so anxious about it and I was absolutely wrecked when I got there.

When I left the gym that morning I felt as if someone had given me a million pounds – it was the sense of achievement, the fact that I'd been understood, the fact that I'd been able to do some work in a gym, and that I now had somewhere to go every Monday and Wednesday. I also had something to work towards – a goal – plus good support and a nice environment to go to.

Mentally, emotionally, psychologically and socially it was the best treatment I'd been given. It was like a club – the exercise referral people would give each other support and encouragement. There were people who'd had coronary operations, people with MS, people who'd had accidents and were doing rehab – everybody would come in and, whatever their ailment, they'd work out and be normal among other people who were doing the same. There was a huge sense of community. And the emphasis was positive – on getting well, getting fit, overcoming problems. At the gym they supported and encouraged me from the start. I think the exercise itself was around 20 per cent of it – the rest was getting into the habit of turning out twice a week – doing something physical, interacting with people.

It changed my world. I started rollerblading on a Sunday, I found a swimming club, and someone to play tennis with. And that all enabled me to have the confidence to go forward and find a part-time job. None of that would have been possible without Active Lifestyles.

Quiz – Find the perfect workout...

Whether you're a gym member, yoga enthusiast or prefer the great outdoors, the type of exercise you do is extremely important when it comes to keeping and staying in shape, and ultimately being happy. Find an exercise routine you love and it won't feel like a chore.

1. You're driving to an unfamiliar destination and become lost. Do you:

a) Keep driving, hoping that you'll eventually find your way?

b) Call ahead for directions?

c) Pull into a petrol station and reassess your bearings?

d) Look on the map for the quickest route to your destination?

2. You have unexpectedly been left some money from a long-lost relative. Do you:

a) Spend, spend, spend!

b) See your financial adviser to find out the best ways to invest it?

c) Put it in your savings account until you decide what to splurge on?

d) Read the financial pages and study the stock market to find out where you'll be able to make the highest return?

3. You've just won a week's holiday of your choice. Do you:

a) Book your dream break to sun-drenched Barbados with your partner?

b) Take yourself on a hiking expedition in Nepal?

c) Spend a week in a luxury health farm?

d) Book an all-inclusive holiday where you'll windsurfing and learn tennis?

4. When you get stressed and angry you:

a) Hit or throw something?

b) Take a few deep breaths and try to figure out what is really bothering you?

c) Ignore it and keep working hard?

d) Do something nice to cheer yourself up?

5. Your ideal weekend would be to:

a) Go to Wimbledon or watch your favourite team play?

b) Eat at the hippest restaurant that all your friends are raving about?

to suit your personality

c) Catch up on your reading?

d) Attend a workshop to learn a new skill?

6. *You feel that you've had a good workout when:*

a) You're sweating profusely and can't speak directly afterwards?

b) You've burnt off a set number of calories?

c) What workout? You'd rather have a hot bath and early night to unwind?

d) Your body feels strong, stretched and de-stressed?

7. *Your perfect partner is someone who:*

a) Likes trying all the latest in foods and sports?

b) Prefers having a civilized dinner at a top restaurant?

c) Enjoys the country and going on rambling walks?

d) Is passionate about books, movies or politics?

8. *The reason you exercise is to (apart from weight loss and general fitness):*

a) Discover something new and exciting about yourself and others?

b) To meet new people who are as health-conscious as yourself?

c) To de-stress and relax your mind and body?

d) To feel empowered within your body?

9. *You admire people who are:*

a) Self-made success stories or entrepreneurs like Richard Branson?

b) Celebrities who are constantly being scrutinized or photographed?

c) Surrounded by an aura of calm and peacefulness?

d) Compete in the Olympics or make history through a discovery?

10. *When you're put in charge of an important project at work, you tend to:*

a) Try to think of new, unexpected ways to surprise your peers?

b) Consider all angles and consider each challenge of the project?

c) Work on it by yourself: you find it quicker and easier that way?

d) Enlist the help of like-minded colleagues to get the project done as quickly and efficiently as possible?

Results

How did you do? There are no right or wrong answers in the quiz, all it does is help determine what sort of personality type you are.

Mostly As: The exercise enthusiast

You're willing to try anything once, whether it's travelling to an unexplored region, or sampling an unfamiliar dish. You're happiest surrounded by people, working on several projects at once. You love exercising and working out, especially when you can feel immediate results.

Your ideal exercise

Cardiovascular and strength-training exercises will help to maintain your energy levels and keep your mind focused. With your unbridled enthusiasm, you may be prone to overtraining and causing injury, so start slowly and build up your strength and resistance gradually. Work with a personal trainer to determine the level of intensity and to set realistic goals for yourself.

Strength training is an ideal way to lose weight, increase your immunity and ward off degenerative diseases. Make sure you eat little and often, so that you're not depleting your energy stores. Being such an inquisitive, creative soul, you may have trouble turning off at night, so make sure you take time to relax.

Mostly Bs: The slow and steady exerciser

You like to consider the pros and cons before you commit yourself to anything. Because of this, you may find it difficult to fully emerge yourself into one particular activity.

Your ideal exercise

You may prefer exercising on your own, so swimming, running or cycling are ideal for you. Swimming is a great total-body workout that builds stamina and burns around 260 calories per half hour. Aquatic exercise is also ideal if you've suffered from some previous sporting injury, as it offers no resistance to the body. For jogging enthusiasts, make sure you've got a comfortable and supportive pair of trainers and that you've drunk enough liquid. If your joints are feeling the strain of all that pavement-pounding, try walking instead. A brisk walk around the park will help clear your head as well as tone up your legs and buttocks. The best way to maintain a workout plan is to set yourself weekly goals. You'll be more likely to stick to something if you've got an obtainable end goal in sight.

Mostly Cs: The emotional exerciser

You cry at soppy movies and are constantly amazed by the beauty of the world. However, when it comes to expressing your own emotions, you may tend to bottle everything up inside, which can lead to digestion and stomach troubles. At the end of a stressful day at work, you will enjoy relaxing, non-combative sports.

Your ideal exercise

Yoga, tai chi or Pilates are ideal for you. The deep-abdominal breathing and slow, controlled movements will help you to release any stress-related tension and are also ideal for improving posture, digestion and circulation. Because these exercises are unlikely to raise your heartbeat, add some cardiovascular workouts to ensure you're burning fat and keeping your heart healthy. A brisk walk in the park is ideal and will help lower your stress levels as well.

Mostly Ds: The all-rounder exerciser

You like to be challenged and inspired by your work and your workouts. Whether it's the great outdoors, or a hard spinning class (aerobics on a bike), your only pre-requisite is that you feel you've achieved something from your fitness.

Your ideal exercise

Social sports would be ideal for you, as they'll give you the opportunity to socialize with other groups and types of people while working up a sweat. The secret of your fitness success is its variety. Joining a gym is probably the best option for you, as the wide range of classes will keep you interested. Varying your exercise routine from day to day is recommended. Not only will you be getting a full-body workout, but you'll be more likely to stick to your exercise programme as you won't get bored.

Sleep

Around seven million Britons are afflicted regularly with insomnia; with one in five of us suffering from a severe lack of sleep. And while another fifth of the population say they sleep just fine, by rising early or going to bed late – thanks to family or job demands – in reality they're still not getting nearly enough snooze time.

Sleep is a biological need, much like food and water. If totally deprived of shut-eye, humans ultimately perish. Yet millions of people are increasingly missing out on, or forgoing their sleep in order to get more done. Today, on average we sleep one hour less per night than we did 20 to 30 years go. Sleep experts say the average adult requires seven to eight hours per night and that anything less may be harmful to health. Some people need more and that's perfectly normal for them. Others can sleep less and wake up completely refreshed.

If you're getting enough sleep your slumbers will be uninterrupted and you will feel well-rested and ready to go when you wake. Most importantly, you should generally have no sleepiness during the day, even when involved in boring or mundane activities. If you're feeling drowsy during the day, you may not have had enough quality sleep.

One of the problems we face today is that we are constantly poised to be receiving or sending information and we may have more household gadgets than we can actually use. We may have dishwashers to clean our dishes, but instead of utilizing those precious saved 15 minutes in relaxation time, we check our email, pay bills, or catch up on office work. This constant on-the-go attitude has to affect our lives somewhere and it's usually in the amount of time we sleep. This lack of sleep can affect you in several ways:

- Lack of concentration throughout the day
- Fatigue, especially around 3 or 4pm
- Weight gain
- Irritability or mood swings
- Lowered immune system

Sleep and mood

Researchers at Rush-Presbyterian-St Luke's Medical Centre in Chicago found that during the time you sleep, your dreams work to improve your mood. They found that people who'd been in neutral moods before nodding off saw little change in attitude when they woke. Subjects who were generally not depressed but went to bed in a bad mood, however, reported feeling much better after a good night's sleep.

This change was reflected in their dreams: people whose disposition improved overnight reported experiencing more negative dreams at the beginning of the night and progressively fewer and fewer as sleep went on. Subjects in neutral moods saw no change in the content of their dreams.

Sleep also helps us in less visible ways. During sleep, the body secretes a hormone that repairs and regenerates tissue throughout the body. Sleep may also be instrumental in reinforcing our memories and, some experts believe, is essential in processing complex emotions.

The types of sleep you need

In healthy sleep, we experience different patterns and – just as important – we experience them in a particular sequence. Non-rapid eye movement (NREM) is the longest period of sleep, when our brain activity and bodily functions slow down. Rapid-eye movement (REM) happens in brief spurts of increased activity in the brain and body. REM is considered the dreaming stage of sleep.

Healthy sleep, then, is when you achieve a certain sequence of sleep stages. This involves about 80 minutes of NREM sleep, followed by about 10 minutes of REM sleep. This 90-minute cycle is repeated four to six times each night. If the sequence is interrupted (for example, by external noise or a sleep disorder), the quality of your sleep suffers.

How can you help yourself?

First, you need to work out what's keeping you awake at night. Biologically, stress is a fact of life. In times past, stress hormones enabled us to hunt, and to survive in the face of danger. Scientists say that it's necessary – even healthy – to have some stress in our lives, but we must maintain control over it. Today, our bodies rarely have time to rest and so we carry

Happy tip

If you suffer from insomnia, try eating a banana about 30 minutes before going to bed. Ripe bananas may raise mood and help you go to sleep. They're believed to have a soothing effect on the body by stimulating serotonin production.

inflated levels of adrenalin within our systems for long periods. Excessive stress can cause heart disease, an impaired immune system, digestive problems, anxiety, depression and feelings of helplessness or anger.

Taking time to relax is as important as eating well. A relaxed body deflects illness and heals faster than one that is addled with stress. Relaxation prevents tension and pain, as the muscles are no longer bunched like clenched fists. Best of all, a relaxed body and mind shows in the face, making you look healthier and more revitalized. You not only appear younger, but act younger too, as your body recovers energy that is normally channelled toward dealing with stress. However, relaxation can be more than a few hours in front of the television after work, and drinking a couple of glasses of wine before collapsing into bed. True relaxation time is quiet, calm time – just for you. It doesn't necessarily have to be hours of meditative silence: even a five-minute relaxation break can do you, your body, and your mind the world of good.

Try these breathing and meditation exercises to improve your chances of a good night's sleep:

Breathing

- Place one hand on your chest and the other on your navel.
- Take a deep breath. If the lower hand doesn't move, you're not breathing deeply enough.
- As you breathe in, feel your abdomen rise and your fingertips part.

Whenever you feel stressed, take time to check your breathing. If you've moved the focus of your breathing back to your chest area, spend time correcting your breathing technique. Eventually, you'll find it natural to breathe correctly; it just takes time and practice.

Meditation

- Sit or lie comfortably.
- Close your eyes and begin the breathing exercises above.
- Allow your thoughts to release. It may help to focus on one thing so that your mind doesn't wander. Try counting: with the first out-breath, count one, the next breath, two, and so on, up to 10.

● Whenever your mind wanders, go back to one and start counting again.
● If you find it impossible to still your mind when your eyes are closed, try this method: light a candle and stare into the centre of the flame. Blink when necessary and let your breathing be calm and steady.

Daily meditation is a powerful tool to help you manage stress. It is important for wellbeing, helping to lower blood pressure, reduce stress and eliminate fine lines and wrinkles. Meditating for as little as five minutes a day can be beneficial, but where possible aim for 20 minutes for a total mind massage.

Top tips for a perfect night's sleep

1. Get up at the same time every day – even at the weekends. Yes, it's hard to set your alarm at 7am on a Saturday or Sunday, but your body will thank you for it. And you don't have to get moving. Make a cup of tea and spend an hour or so reading that book you've been meaning to get round to.

2. Open the curtains. Your body needs to get sunshine or light at the same time every day, so that it can release serotonin signals to your brain. Your body clock will also create a sleep/wake cycle and regular routine.

3. If you can't get to sleep at night after about 30 minutes, don't force the issue. Do something relaxing instead, such as reading or listening to music. Don't berate yourself about not being able to sleep; instead say, 'I can't do anything about this right now.' Repeat this over and over, until your mind slowly relaxes and you drift into sleep.

4. If you do have to get up, try to keep your surroundings as dark as possible – some research suggests that you should keep 'night as night'; switching on the light fools your brain into thinking it's time to get up.

5. Try a relaxation technique: Lie on your back, with your arms to your sides, palms up. Starting with your feet, gently flex each muscle and then release. Imagine that each part of your body is sinking into velvet darkness. Work all the way up your body until all your muscles are relaxed, before emptying your mind of thoughts.

6. If your mind races with everything you have to do, don't stay awake mulling over what can't be dealt with. Instead, write it all down. Don't try to think of solutions. Simply writing down your concerns will help you stop worrying about them.

7. Remember how as a child you used to be read to until you fell asleep? This 'downtime' is just as necessary now. Every night try to follow a similar pattern, whether it's a warm bath, cleansing and pampering your face, getting your clothes ready for the next day, or reading for about 30 minutes before trying to go to sleep.

8. Reserve your bedroom for sex and sleep only. Don't take paperwork to bed to go over, or use your laptop whilst under the covers. Separate your two worlds as much as possible.

9. If nothing is working, try herbal sleep tablets or homeopathic remedies. Always make sure that you take pills, syrups and remedies as instructed on the packaging. Check with your GP or pharmacist if you have any doubts.

Making work work

The way you earn your money says more about you than you realize. Are you happy with a 9–5 job, with no prospects, just as long as you're paid each month? Or are you constantly on the lookout for the Next Big Thing? There's no right or wrong, just what works for you. As an Australian, I've been brought up to believe that you should work to live, not live to work.

If time is your enemy

If you never have enough hours in the day to get your work done, then it's time you took a look at your organizational skills. Do you?

● Take on more work than is humanly possible to achieve?
● Have problems saying 'no' to your boss?
● Wake up in the morning with a feeling of dread because you have to go into the office?
● Constantly cancel plans with friends or family due to work commitments?
● Take your gym bag to work on a Monday and find it there untouched on a Friday?
● Get stressed on Sunday about the week ahead?

If you've answered 'yes' to even just one of these questions, it's time to redress your work/life balance.

Achieving the work/life balance

Let's face it. We'd all love to live on a deserted island, with the only task on our to-do list being 'Get more sunscreen'. It's a nice dream but we'd also be stark raving mad after six months. OK, 12 months.

So, back to reality. Work is an integral part of your life and there's nothing wrong with making work your life, as long as that's how you really want it to be. We spend the majority of our waking hours in work mode, so it makes sense to do what makes us happy. And this is the crux. For many of us, joining the circus, being an international model, or the head of a conglomerate is just not realistic. But that doesn't mean that you can't make your dreams a part of the life that you are living.

Integrating your work with your dreams

Close your eyes. Think about the last time you were happy? Were you entertaining friends over a sumptuous dinner? Were you advising a friend on a health concern? Rock climbing? Or organizing a celebratory party?

Whatever you were doing, could you imagine doing this and getting paid for it? Could you train as a chef? A nutritionist or counsellor? Work part-time at your local climbing centre or set up your own business as a party planner? What you love doing is an extension of you, your personality and your heart, so why not research some ways to make your life your work?

Taking responsibility

Being happy at work comes down to whether or not you feel appreciated, and whether or not you have enough time in the day to spend on yourself. It's your responsibility to make sure your approach to work is a healthy one. Try this:

- When you plan your week's work, ask yourself, is it realistic? If not, speak up. Offer a solution, not a problem to your boss, such as, 'I'll finish 80 per cent of X this week and the remainder by next Wednesday. If it needs to be done by Friday, I know of a freelancer who can come in for a couple of days to help out.'

- Always leave work on time. Book your appointments: whether it's the gym, to see friends, catch a movie or have a massage, and put them in your diary. These appointments are just as important as your day-to-day meetings. Don't let yourself down.

- Don't take it personally. One of the biggest reasons we're unhappy at work is because we're stuck in the fear cycle. Fear that we'll be fired, fear that someone else will be promoted instead. There's no such thing as the perfect job or company. It's up to you to make the best of your current situation.

- Take regular breaks. Use some of your holiday time and enjoy a long weekend every now and then. A three-day weekend feels decadent, but it can be a necessity. Whatever you're working on in the office will be there when you get back and when you do, you'll be a much happier, relaxed employee who can complete the task in less time.

Making relationships work

Being in a relationship can be exhilarating, exciting and, let's face it, exhausting. Being on your own can be completely fulfilling, fun and sometimes lonely. As most of us know, it's possible to feel just as lonely in a relationship as it can be staying in on a Saturday night with only the remote control and your cat for company.

Whether you're in a relationship, starting one, or are looking for one, it's imperative to remember one very important fact: a relationship will not make you happy. I know it sounds trite, but as with many trite sayings, it's true. You may have somebody to do things with and someone to confide in, and yes, these are special, intimate advantages of being in love. But you're still the same person you were before. So, if you have trouble saying 'no' to others, you're still going to have the same problem, even though you have somebody at your side. If you get terrible PMT, you'll still get it once a month! Being in a relationship shouldn't complete you (no matter what the movies say), but it should complement you.

Relationship know-how

- Be honest with yourself and your partner. It's not their fault you had a rotten day, so don't take it out on them. Instead, act responsibly and go to the gym or take a brisk walk and get your frustrations or stress out in a positive way.
- Don't stay in a damaging relationship because you're afraid of being alone and think that you'll never meet anybody. You probably will meet somebody else, and if you don't, so what? Ask most people in a relationship and they'll tell you they miss their old 'single' self. So, however long your singleness lasts, take advantage of it. Get into new habits. When you do start your next relationship you'll be a much happier, stronger person, who's less likely to repeat the same mistakes.
- Consider counselling. If you're facing the same old problems with each partner, don't blame it all on them. After all, what do all your ex's have in common? Yep, it's you. As I mentioned before, only YOU can change. Counselling can help you determine what your relationship trigger points are and how to reprogramme them.

Happy tip

Feeling down? Give your partner a kiss. A study found that women who were in happy relationships kissed their partners every day. So pucker up!

● Don't have an affair. Many people think that happiness can be gained from outside of their current relationship. If you're truly unhappy act like a grown-up and finish it. You may hurt that person for a short while, but they'll get over it. Getting over a betrayal is much harder.

● Remember that your partner is also meant to be your best friend, and act accordingly. You wouldn't shout and scream and throw something at your best friend, would you? So why treat your partner like that? We're all guilty of treating our partners badly, and yes, forgiveness is what being in a relationship is all about. Be nice.

Home is your haven

Your home is more than bricks and mortar. It's your space where you feel safe to relax, to entertain friends or to hide away from the world. We all know that feeling when we walk into our home and immediately feel better. It's not because it's beautifully decorated or because it's immaculately tidy… it's because of an emotion that the surroundings give.

There are many ways a home can impart emotion: through furnishings, smells, decorations and colour. Most of us wouldn't feel too comfortable in a home that has black painted walls, plastered with disturbing images, whilst trying to not breathe too deeply due to the noxious fumes! Whereas an airy house, with light coloured walls, flowers throughout, a warm smell of baking bread and not too much clutter immediately makes most people feel at home.

There are several reasons for this. For example, a smell can invoke memories of a childhood home, happy days or a holiday.

What is colour therapy?

It is colour that has the strongest effect on your moods. Colour therapy uses the energy of different light waves to balance and heal the body. Although it is invisible to the naked eye, natural sunlight contains all colours of the spectrum: red, orange, yellow, green, blue, indigo and violet. It bathes us in a sea of colour, which can be seen when light is split with a prism or water from the atmosphere to create a rainbow.

A colour therapist will pinpoint imbalances in the energy vibrations of your cells and then use colour vibrations to correct those imbalances and restore wellbeing. Most therapists use a colour, together with its complement (the hue that is opposite in the spectrum and balancing in its qualities and effects). The therapist may ask you to pick three cards from a selection of eight and the colours you choose will reveal your current emotional and physical state. These colours may then be used along with their complementary shades to help balance your vibrational health. Vibrational health is the rate at which energy levels move. If your vibrational levels are high, you are probably feeling energetic and positive with ideas and plans. If your levels are low, you may be feeling lethargic and teary. To assist the process, a special device may be used to beam coloured light on to your body.

In addition, the therapist may also encourage you to visualize certain colours, channel colour to you through his or her hands, advise you on which colours to wear (such as putting a base layer of white clothing underneath outer colours to filter out unwanted colour vibrations), which coloured foods and even drinks you should choose.

How does colour affect our emotions?

All living things vibrate at their own frequency, including colours. It makes sense, then, that we will react in a certain way to a particular colour. How do you feel when you put on a bright red top? Ready to take on the world? What about a white, floaty kaftan? Relaxed and serene? Here is a quick guide to healing colours:

Blue
Healing powers Shades of blue are restful and can be used to help lower blood pressure, improve sleep and to reduce pain perception.
Best used In bathrooms. Wear blue when you want to be treated gently.

Red
Healing powers Gives feelings of empowerment, encourages sensuality.
Best used In living rooms or bedrooms. Wear red when you have a job interview or a difficult meeting.

Green

Healing powers Calms and reduces anxiety and tension. It's believed that if a person is recovering from stress or ill-health a natural setting that contains green foliage will accelerate the healing process.
Best used Pale green is a restful colour for bedrooms or for hallways. Wear green when you want to feel grounded and at peace.

Orange

Healing powers Stimulates emotional, physical and sexual energy.
Best used Use sparingly in living rooms or bedrooms. A good idea is to accessorize the room with orange glass vases to infuse it with sunlight. Wear orange when you want to lift your spirits.

Yellow

Healing powers Promotes clear thinking, self-control, optimism, inner strength and helps to resolve unaddressed emotions and feelings.
Best used Yellow in the kitchen creates a happy family atmosphere. A yellow top on a winter's day will remind you of the sunshine!

Turquoise

Healing powers Increases your emotional resistance, boosts immunity and protects you from the influences and demands of others.
Best used Mimic the ocean and paint your bathroom walls turquoise. Turquoise jewellery can add a feeling of freshness and vitality.

Violet

Healing powers Calms and helps to encourage sleep.
Best used A violet room can be very relaxing and feminine. Wear violet when you know your day is going to be busy.

Holistic health

The world of alternative medicines has slowly become recognized as a useful part of a wellbeing programme. Doctors now recommend acupuncture, craniology, homeopathy and a whole host of other therapies for many ailments. To help improve your mood, there's nothing better than putting yourself in the hands of a qualified practitioner of one of these many therapies.

Acupuncture

Acupuncture is increasingly being used by people suffering from depression. It has a long history of use in the treatment of psychiatric disorders in China and is now being used both on its own and in conjunction with other therapies, such as psychotherapy and anti-depressants. In 1998 the World Health Organization recommended acupuncture as a proven treatment for depression – a symbol of acceptance and recognition.

Acupuncture is an Eastern therapy that aims to improve the overall wellbeing of the patient, rather than treating specific symptoms in isolation. Traditional Chinese philosophy states that our health is dependent on the body's motivating energy – known as Qi – moving in a smooth and balanced way through a series of meridians (channels) beneath the skin.

For any number of reasons, Qi may become unbalanced and lead to illness. By inserting fine needles into the channels of energy or Qi, an acupuncturist can stimulate the body's own healing response and help restore its natural balance.

A recent study found that acupuncture brought significant clinical improvement to depression sufferers. It was found to be especially good for treating anxiety symptoms.

Acupressure

Less intrusive than acupuncture (there are no needles!), acupressure is performed by applying steady, firm pressure on specific points along the body. If you prefer, you can rub on the acupressure point briskly to stimulate it rather than just applying pressure. When stimulated, these spots – which are identical to acupuncture points – correspond to and affect other parts of the body.

According to Chinese medicine, depression can occur when you repress certain emotions, such as anger or guilt. Using antidepression acupressure points can help to release this blocked energy. Once it is free to rise to the surface, you can examine these feelings and try to gain a greater understanding of them. Acupressure is useful in alleviating many of the physical symptoms as well as the sluggishness of mild depression.

Located at the top of your head are three points which, when pressed, can help relieve the symptoms of mild depression and lift your mood. The fourth point is located below your knee. Try these simple acupressure exercises:

Point one

Place your left thumb on the top of your left ear and your right thumb on the top of your right ear. Move your fingertips towards the top of your head and feel for a hollow near the top centre of your head. Place your middle finger in the centre, and position your fingers one inch either side of your middle finger. These points are also pressure points to help lift your mood. Apply firm pressure to these points for about 30 seconds, relaxing your body, and let tension slip away.

Point two

The two hollows at the base of your neck muscles are also guilty of storing tension and emotions. Most people tend to rub this area when they're stressed. Press these areas hard for 15 seconds, then release. This will help relieve irritability, exhaustion and stress.

Point three

Press the point between your eyebrows in the groove where the bridge of your nose meets your forehead for about 30 seconds. Pressing this point can soothe your emotions and relieves depression.

Point four

Clasp your hand just under your knee cap, placing your fingers so that they're an inch outside of your shinbone. Press all fingers down firmly for about 30 seconds. These points are helpful for emotional balance, and relieving fatigue and depression.

Massage

Massage is the kneading and stroking of the body's soft tissues – the skin and muscles – with varying degrees of pressure. It is incorporated in a number of traditional Eastern health systems such as Ayurveda and Chinese medicine. Practitioners of modern complementary therapies, such as aromatherapy and reflexology, use various massage techniques.

What does it do?

Gentle massage affects the nervous system through the nerve endings in the skin, stimulating the release of endorphins, the body's natural 'feel-good' chemical, to help induce relaxation and a sense of wellbeing, and also relieve pain and reduce levels of stress chemicals such as cortisol and noradrenaline. It helps reverse the damaging effects of stress by slowing heart rate, respiration and metabolism, and by lowering blood pressure.

Stronger massage stimulates blood circulation to improve the supply of oxygen and nutrients to body tissues and helps the lymphatic system to flush away waste products. It eases tense and knotted muscles and stiff joints, improving mobility and flexibility. The most common massage techniques include:

- *Effleurage* – a fluid, sweeping stroke, which can be used with varying degrees of pressure
- *Petrissage* – firm kneading and rolling of the tissues
- *Frottage (or friction)* – deep, direct pressure on areas of muscle tension
- *Percussion* – tapping and cupping over muscles and fleshy parts

Massage is now used more frequently in conventional healthcare to relieve anxiety, reduce pain, and to help patients with cancer, AIDS and heart problems. Over 90 per cent of UK hospices offer some form of touch-based therapy. It is often available in drug rehabilitation and pain clinics, and increasingly through NHS GP practices. Family members are taught to give simple massage to seriously ill or dying friends and relatives.

How does it work?

Touch is our first sensual experience and remains, along with smell, the most immediate and evocative link between mind and body. The skin is the body's largest sensory organ and thousands of specialized receptors in the dermis, the second layer of skin, react to external stimuli such as heat, cold and pressure by sending messages through the nervous system to the brain. Massage is said to increase the activity of the vagus nerve, one of 12 cranial nerves, which affects the secretion of food absorption hormones as well as heart rate and respiration.

What is it good for?

Studies at the Touch Research Institute at the University of Miami, Florida, have shown that massage reduces anxiety and depression, relieves back pain and muscle pain, lowers high blood pressure, eases PMT symptoms, re-energises stressed office workers and boosts the immune system to better fight infection. A recent multi-centre study in the American Medical Association's Annals of Internal Medicine showed that therapeutic massage was an effective treatment for persistent lower back pain, out-performing acupuncture.

Massage is generally safe, but there are some cautions:

- Massage of the abdomen should be avoided in the first three months of pregnancy.
- Consult a doctor before having a massage if you are pregnant, have phlebitis, thrombosis, varicose veins, acute back pain, epilepsy, cancer, a personality disorder, psychotic illness or any undiagnosed pain, lumps or bumps.
- Do not have a massage if you have a fever or any infectious diseases.

Types of massage

There are various different forms of massage to try. Most therapists are skilled in a number of types – it's best to discuss your health and emotional needs before you begin a massage treatment.

Ayurvedic massage

Ayurvedic is a system of health and medicine used in India. Ayurveda means 'life knowledge' or 'right living'. The basic theory is that there are three main body types or (called doshas), and each dosha should be treated in a different way. Ayurvedic massage treats energy channels called marmas (similar to meridians). It is believed the body has around 100 marmas, which contain the vital life force and energy.

Cranio-sacral therapy

This is a technique that aims to correct cerebral and spinal imbalances and blockages to improve the functioning of the central nervous system. This involves working with the soft tissues, membranes, energy and cerebral fluids surrounding the cranium, spine and sacrum. It is believed that there is a rhythm flowing through the body, which can give distinct information about the health and functioning of the entire body. By monitoring the cranio-sacral rhythm through palpation (subtle touch by the practitioner), the therapist can locate the part of the body that may be holding physical or emotional trauma. Once identified, gentle compression and stretching stimulates the body to make corrections and readjustments in the form of physical movements or emotional release.

Deep tissue massage

This is a form of deep-pressure massage designed to reach the core layers of the body, often using the elbows as well as the usual thumbs, fingers and fists. Deep tissue work helps with chronic pain and injury rehabilitation. A therapist should take a full case history from a client before embarking on deep tissue massage. Always make sure that your masseur is accredited, as injury can occur from incorrect technique.

Hawaiian/Lomi-Lomi massage

Originating from the Hawaiian Islands, Lomi-Lomi is one of the most beautiful forms of massage treatments as it looks more like a dance performed by the practitioner than a massage technique. A session usually begins with the practitioner asking the client what results they want from the session. The massage technique itself consists of graceful, sweeping arm movements and ceremonial music. The elbows and forearms are used, along with the fingertips.

Zero balancing

Developed by Fritz Smith in 1975, this type of massage works to align the physical body with the energetic body. Treatments are done with the client fully clothed and you begin the treatment in a seated position, progressing to a reclining position. The skeletal system is the main focus of the treatment as this is where the deepest and strongest currents of energy exist.

Quick self-massage

There's nothing lovelier than a massage, but if you're short on time, cash or just can't get an appointment, there's still hope. It is possible to give yourself a massage. It will reconnect you with your entire body, by allowing your mind to refocus on everything below your neck!

Start with your head and work your way down to your toes.

1. Pour some massage oil onto your palms and, using flat hands, rub the oil vigorously into your hair and scalp. Add an uplifting aromatherapy oil, such as Melissa, lemon, peppermint or rose.
2. Use your fingertips to cover your head with small circular movements.
3. Gently massage your face and ears and then your neck.
4. Knead your shoulders and vigorously massage your arms, with up-and-down motions. Use circular movements on your elbows and knead your hands and fingers.
5. Massage your chest and stomach using large gentle circular motions. Massage your sides and back. Try to do this without twisting or straining your back.
6. Use vigorous up- and-down motions on your legs, with circular movements at your knees and ankles.
7. Massage the tops and bottoms of your feet and use your fingers to massage your toes.
8. Once you're finished, take a few minutes to relax and enjoy the sensation of feeling awakened. Then take a warm shower and wash off the oils.
9. Drink a large glass of water to help combat dehydration.

Homeopathy

If you are experiencing a transient, rather than chronic, depression, homeopathic remedies can be useful in alleviating the blues. Homeopathy works by treating like with like. For instance, if you have hayfever, a homeopath will give you pills to take, which actually contain small amounts of pollen. This is to remind your body to fight the foreign bodies and therefore boost immunity, moods and healing powers.

A homeopathic pill is made up of the active ingredient in question, diluted many times, and a 'carrier' substance, usually sucrose. The strength or potency of a pill is described with the letter 'c'. If the remedy says 100c on the label, it is stronger than one that says 6c. The stronger the remedy, the more it has been diluted. If you see an 'x', this indicates a weaker potency. Homoeopathy is generally safe and does not interfere with other medicines. It's ideal for young children and even animals.

When taking a remedy, avoid touching it with your fingers, as this can destroy the potency. Instead, tip the white pillule first into the lid of the bottle and then place under the tongue where it will dissolve. Don't eat anything 20 minutes before or after taking the remedy.

The following remedies and dosages are ideal for those suffering from low moods or mild depression. Ideally, visit a homeopath for a consultation. The homeopath may suggest dietary changes to help aid your emotional healing.

Ignatia is often prescribed for depression caused by grief, where the symptoms are wildly fluctuating moods and inappropriate behaviour, such as bursting into tears or laughing for no reason.

Pulsatilla is recommended for depression caused by hormonal changes, when you cry at the slightest provocation and want a lot of reassurance and attention.

Sepia is useful if you feel depressed and irritable, dragged down by responsibilities and worries.

Arsenicum is good if you are restless, chilly, exhausted, and obsessively neat and tidy.

Aurum is useful if you feel totally worthless and disgusted with yourself.

Flower remedies

Flower remedies are useful in dealing with a number of conditions often associated with mild depression. They work by stimulating the body's own capacity to heal itself, by balancing negative feelings, helping you to take control, recover from shock or an upsetting experience, and kick-starting your motivation. There are several types of flower remedies, Bach, Australian Bush Flower, Californian, to name a few. Ideally, visit a healer who will either make you a bespoke remedy or recommend an all-encompassing remedy.

Agrimony is recommended if you tend to maintain a smiling appearance while suffering inner anguish and despair.

Centaury is helpful for depression accompanied by feelings of intimidation.

Cherry Plum relieves feelings of fearfulness, whether of things real or imagined.

Gorse may help if you have a sense of hopelessness.

Honeysuckle is helpful for those whose thoughts dwell on happier times past.

Mustard is useful for sadness and feelings of ineffectuality.

Rescue Remedy is the first choice to ease acute anxiety. It contains a combination of:

Star of Bethlehem – helps trauma and shock.

Clematis – prevents tendency to 'pass out' and lapse into unconsciousness; helps if you are not feeling present mentally.

Cherry Plum – helps combat anger, the fear of the mind giving way, and that you are on the verge of a breakdown.

Impatiens – helps ease irritability, tension and fidgetiness.

Rock Rose is recommended for frozen terror and panic.

Sweet chestnut will help if you have feelings of bleakness and despair.

Walnut is useful for depression that results from difficulty in adjusting to change.

Wild Rose is beneficial for people who have lost interest in life, become apathetic and have stopped caring about anything.

Willow is good for depression caused by resentment.

Happy tip

Try the flower remedy Revitalise. It contains olive, which is good for recharging low batteries, and crab apple and walnut, which work together to help you get back in contact with yourself if you're feeling detached or overwhelmed by outside influences.

Aromatherapy

Sniff a bad smell and you'll experience an emotional reaction: disgust, nausea or even a memory. A warm comforting smell, such as baking bread, however, conjures up feelings and memories of happy, sunny mornings. Aromatherapy works in just this way – by prompting a chemical change in the brain.

Aromatherapy uses aromatic essences extracted from plants. These extracted oils are the plant's hormones – the most vital substance of the plant. Essential oils should never be used directly on the skin. Instead, add them to a base oil or cream. Recommended base oils include sweet almond, sunflower and grapeseed. Some essential oils (such as lemon) are too strong to add undiluted to a bath. Various oils affect you in different ways. Take a look at the table to see which oil is for you:

NB: Some oils can counteract homeopathic remedies, so be sure to check with a homeopath if you are using both treatments simultaneously.

Cardamom
Good for Feeling tired, exhausted or run down
When to use it Wintertime
How to use it To ward off colds and flu, mix 4 drops each of rose and tea tree oil with 2 drops of cardamom oil and 5ml of base oil. Add to your bath.

Clary sage
Good for When you're feeling blue. Also helps relieve symptoms of PMT.
When to use it In the mornings
How to use it Mix 12 drops of clary sage, 10 drops of geranium and 3 drops of rose oil with 50ml of base carrier oil. Apply in a circular motion to your stomach.

Jasmine
Good for Lifting the spirits
When to use it At night
How to use it For an indulgent bath, mix 3 drops of jasmine oil into almond or grapeseed oil or half a cup of full-fat milk. Add to your bath.

Lavender
Good for Insomnia and to calm and soothe
When to use it When you're panicked. Best used at night
How to use it Add 4–8 drops to your bath, or put 2 drops on your pillow to help you sleep.

May chang
Good for Increasing energy levels lifting moods and beating depression
When to use it Anytime you need a lift
How to use it Put 5–6 drops in an oil burner, or put 2 drops of may chang and 2 drops of frankincense oil in your bath for an energizing soak.

Rose
Good for Calming
When to use it Bathtime
How to use it Mix 6 drops of sandalwood, 4 drops of orange and 1 drop of rose oil with a glass of full-fat milk or base carrier oil. Add to your bath.

Rosemary
Good for Stimulating and invigorating. Helps focus
When to use it Daytime
How to use it Mix with a base carrier oil and rub on your hands and feet to help you think clearly.

Why hobbies mean happiness

When you last wrote your CV, what did you put down as your hobbies? Did you struggle to even think of any? Unfortunately, as we get older, we tend fill our lives with other commitments instead of activities we really enjoy. In other words, a life of 'have tos' rather than 'want tos'.

But the 'want tos' are an imperative part of our happiness. Psychologists have figured out that the formula to happiness is: family, friends and hobbies.

Extra-curricular activities provide a great way to escape from the pressures of everyday life: they occupy your mind, provide a social structure, and, depending on the sort of hobby, can help you lose weight and prevent health problems, such as Alzheimer's. A recent study found that people who had several after-work activities or extra-curriculum activities were slimmer than those without such interests. Hardly surprising – if you're playing sport, learning a language, or a special skill, you're less likely to spend your evenings slumped in front of the television.

Learning a new skill excites the mind, fires your enthusiasm and can help restore confidence. Plus, a weekly commitment to attend a class, game or meeting will help provide some structure in your life, which is often something that is lacking in people who are feeling down.

A study in the *New England Journal of Medicine* found that staying mentally active may actually help prevent Alzheimer's disease and other types of dementia. And that doesn't mean that you need to spend your free time solving complicated mathematical equations. Any stimulating activity – playing cards or board games, doing crossword puzzles, reading, going to the museum or art gallery, playing a musical instrument – may minimize age-related memory loss.

How to choose a hobby
What do you want to get out of it?
If the opportunity to meet new people is the most important thing for you, try an activity that demands interaction, such as a language class, dance class or reading group. You may even be hoping to meet a partner. Maximize your chances by choosing a social activity.

If your priority is to do something where you can measure your progress, choose an activity that has precise goals that are measured through tests or exams.

How much time can you afford?

Don't overcommit yourself. If you like at least two quiet nights in each week, then a hobby that takes up every evening will just not work. If your working hours or family commitments are unpredictable, a weekend class may be easier. Don't create more stress for yourself by setting out to do something you don't have the time to do. Whatever you do, think carefully about whether you have a realistic chance of staying with your commitment. The feeling of completing a course, attending a class or winning a game can be more powerful than an antidepressant.

How much money can you spend?

Some activities that you originally thought might be expensive may actually be affordable. Do you need to fork out for materials, books, plus the cost of the course itself, or can you borrow or buy things second-hand? Most public libraries run reading groups and keep enough loan copies of the week's book for everyone. For a walking group all you need is some comfortable clothes and shoes.

Gardening can burn as many calories as an hour's gym class, plus you have the added benefit of creating something beautiful for yourself, your home and the environment.

Painting Tapping into your creative side can help you deal with stress, encourage positive thinking and perhaps help you discover a hidden talent. A solitary hobby, but it can have the benefits of a social group if you are attending a painting course or trip.

Cooking Discovering a new form of cooking, whether it's international cuisine or speciality cakes, is a great form of meditation. Preparing simple everyday meals for yourself or your family can be incredibly rewarding after a tough day.

Happy tip

Can't think of a hobby? Close your eyes and imagine yourself as a child. What made you happy? What hobbies did you have then? Could you pick these up again?

Reading Whether you like to curl up with a book, or love discussing the latest novel from your favourite author, reading is often forgotten as a real hobby. But books can inspire, heal and entertain you. Think about joining a reading group. Whether you go to the park for an hour's uninterrupted reading or visit your favourite café for a coffee, cake and read, treat this hobby as you would any other.

Music Slow, relaxing music helps some people deal with the root causes of their depression, such as anger, frustration, sadness or anxiety. Listening to music for at least 20 minutes each day can help slow your heart rate and help you focus on your feelings. Music is a form of sensory stimulation that provokes responses due to the familiarity, predictability and feelings of security associated with it.

According to The American Music Therapy Association (AMTA), music therapy is an effective and valid treatment for people who have psychosocial, affective, cognitive and communicative needs. Research results and clinical experiences attest to the viability of music therapy even in those who are resistive to other treatments.

Finding your spiritual side

Different forms of spirituality offer comfort in times of suffering and provide a message of hope that gives those who rely on it a buffer against depression and other emotional upheavals.

In a study of 4,000 older Americans (age 65 to 102), researchers at Duke University School of Medicine found that those who attended church at least once a week were half as likely to be depressed as those who attended religious services less frequently. Other studies have shown that religiously inclined people over 60 are healthier and live longer than those who are less spiritual.

If you think that spirituality may be your answer, ask some like-minded friends to take you along to a service. Keep an open mind about which form of spirituality to adopt – Buddhism or Sufism could be what you are looking for, for example. It may take several visits to various different types of religions or faiths before you find one that sits comfortably with you.

Retreats

In an increasingly noisy world, more and more people are heading to places of enforced silence for rest and recuperation. A silent retreat can be beneficial for people who just want to get away from it all. Typically, a silent retreat has a monastic feel. Rooms and food are basic, there is space for praying, meditation, gentle exercise and best of all, peace and quiet. If you are thinking of going on a silent retreat, consider a couple of points first:

● Would you be comfortable in a strict, spartan environment?
● Do you want the retreat to be part of a religious order or are you happy left to your own spiritual thoughts?
● Would you prefer a semi-silent retreat, where there is quiet time allocated each day, with the rest of the time used for group discussion, exercise and activities?
● Do you think you could enjoy a week by yourself without the influence and comfort of others?

If you decide you could cope with all the above, or want to find out if you could, consider finding out more about spiritual retreats.

Case Study

Louise Moon, 37, visited a monastic retreat in Devon for one week.
I'd been working extremely hard and needed some time out. Even though I'm a writer and work primarily at home alone, my head was full of plots and voices, which weren't my own. I decided to visit a retreat on the recommendation of a friend.

The rooms were comfortable, but bare. At first it was difficult not to greet fellow guests – it felt rude to just nod or smile. The first four days I hated it. I felt so lonely and lost without the reassurance of a telephone or email. I went on a long walk and wondered what in the world I had got myself into. Then on the fourth day, something inside me clicked. I woke up and welcomed the silence: around me and inside me. I didn't feel the need to rush around, I just slowed down and did some gentle yoga stretches before sitting under a tree and did nothing. Thoughts did of course come to my mind, but I just let them go. I knew that they'd be there next week.

One thing I did get out of the week was a new story idea. I'd been grappling with an idea for a book for years, and suddenly, towards the end of my stay, it came to me in a flash of clarity. When my week was up, I was nervous about going home, but felt more energetic and happier than I'd felt in years. I was determined to continue to take short retreats for myself – and usually organize one 'quiet' day every six weeks or so. I don't know if I'd go back to the retreat – I learnt a lot there and have continued with my yoga and writing. I'm much better at taking quiet time for myself now, instead of feeling that I have to be involved in everything that's going on around me.

The Seven-day Happy Plan

One of the worst side-effects of feeling down is the lack of motivation and impetus you have to do anything. That's why our monthly plan is easy to follow: there's no difficult standing-on-your head postures that promise happiness and enlightenment – just sensible, straightforward advice. And if you feel that you want to try something quick and easy, each day has a 60-second mood-lifter that will help kick-start your new, happier life.

Follow this plan for 30 days. You can transpose the days – it doesn't matter which order you do them in, as long as you get through all five daily plans each week. Try to follow the plans exactly, but if you slip, don't worry: just restart the next day. Good luck!

Day one

Morning glory

Forget greeting the morning sun. Instead, treat every morning as though it was your birthday. Make a pot of peppermint or your favourite tea, pick up your favourite book or magazine and spend 30 minutes (no longer) back in your cosy bed. Wiggle your toes and allow your mind to focus on the sensation as your body slowly awakens. If you like, turn the radio on, and slowly spend the time allowing your mind to readjust to the new day.

Morning treat

Write down one task you wish to complete today. Don't make it difficult, unobtainable or work- or bill-oriented. Keep it simple. If you're washing your hair today, plan to spend an extra few minutes in the shower applying a hair treatment. It doesn't have to be anything particularly exotic, as long as it makes you feel that little bit extra special.

Breakfast

We all know the importance of a good, wholesome breakfast. If you have the time, try to prepare a weekend-style meal. Try an omelette: mix two eggs and a tablespoon of water. Add some salt and pepper. Pour into a hot pan, lifting the sides occasionally. Grate some Cheddar cheese and place in the middle of the omelette. Fold one side over, to form a calzone. Serve with a glass of orange juice or warm water with lemon juice. This will help flush out toxins in your body, which may add to feelings of lethargy or despondency.

Morning stretch

Time for your shower. I always recommend a shower in the morning. The water needles are invigorating and you can alternate the heat between hot and cold to really get the heart beating! Use your nicest-smelling shower gel and, using a body glove, rub yourself all over. This will help your mind connect to the different parts of your body, even your little toes!
If you can bear it, just before you get out of the shower, turn the hot down and slowly cool the temperature. It will help your skin glow and also give your brain a recognizable sign to wake up and start the day.

Noontime niceties

However busy you are, whatever the weather, go outside for lunch. Just five minutes of natural sunshine a day will do wonders for your spirits. A five-minute walk to a sandwich bar or salad bar will boost your circulation and help clear your mind if you've been focusing for hours. Plus, you've managed to fit in 10 minutes of exercise. For lunch, choose something filling, but not stodgy. Try swapping your usual sandwich for soup, salad and fruit, or change your potato topping from cheese to tuna. This way, your body will be using the energy from these foods for the next few hours, so you'll be more awake than if you'd had a nap-inducing bowl of pasta or a carb-laden sandwich.

60-second mood-lifter

Your brain uses 20 per cent of the oxygen in your body. If you're feeling bored and lethargic, five deep, slow breaths will do wonders at boosting your mood and energy levels.

Zzz-time

No, it's not bedtime, but it feels like it! It's 3pm, and you're likely to be feeling tired. If you're at home, then lie down. A 20-minute nap will refresh your mind and body. If you're at work, then go for a quick walk: go to the corner shop and buy that birthday card for your friend. Or make a cup of herbal tea and spend some time cleaning up your desk. It may sound mundane, but you'll feel fresher and clearer – on your desk and in your head.

After-work wind down

Going to the gym after work can be one of the most difficult appointments to keep, but if you've promised yourself that you'll go then try to do it. After all, if you had promised to meet a friend you wouldn't stand them up would you? You don't have to run yourself ragged on the treadmill or work your abs, tum and bum. A gentle swim, followed by a steam or sauna, will help break up your day. Plus, you've managed to do some exercise and get some precious pampering in too! If you're not a member of a gym, then try to walk for at least 10 or 20 minutes before getting your usual bus or train. Don't promise yourself that you'll exercise once you're home, it just won't happen.

Dinner date

Try to eat before 9pm. Most nutritionists recommend eating by 7pm, but in today's busy society this is not always possible. Make a rule and stick to it: the later the time, the lighter the meal. If you like cooking, then you'll know that preparing a meal is a great way to relieve the day's stress and unwind. But if you don't, then it may just seem like a chore. A good way to boost your mood is to make something as simple as possible, such as stir-fry vegetables with wild rice.

After dinner

It's tempting to flop in front of your favourite soap, but just wait. It's not time for sofa slobbing yet. Spend 15 minutes attending to any administration, such as bills to pay, post to be sent, or phone calls to return. Once you've done that? Reward yourself with the remote.

Time for bed

During this week, it's important to establish a routine, so try to stick to a realistic bedtime. Ideally, 10.30 is a good time to begin preparations for the land of nod. If you still feel as if your mind is buzzing, then run a warm bath. Add some essential oils such as rose, clary sage, lavender or camomile. Place a radio in the bathroom and turn on some relaxing music. Light some tea lights and place them around the room. Dim the lights and hop in. Allow your mind to drift. Don't worry if your mind is still full. Allow your thoughts to wash over you as you would a wave in the ocean. Take deep breaths and exhale slowly though your nose. Focus on your body, limb by limb. Do you feel tense? Lower each limb. Is your jaw clenched? Loosen it. Move your attention from your head to your toes, relaxing and releasing tension as you go.

Just before lights out

A good night's sleep – that is, one that's untroubled and worry free – may have been hard to come by. Write down anything from the day that's worrying you or that you didn't manage to do. But instead of saying, 'What I didn't do today,' turn this around to 'What I want to achieve tomorrow'. This way you've acknowledged your worries and your tasks. And now you can go to sleep knowing that you'll tackle them tomorrow.

Day two

Morning glory

Rise and shine! Stretch your body from head to toe, without getting out of bed. Raise your arms above your head, point your toes and s-t-r-e-t-c-h!

Breakfast

Porridge is a great way to start the day. Nutritionists say that people who eat porridge are less likely to be overweight, suffer from Seasonal Affective Disorder or mood swings. Add some golden syrup and blueberries for a sweet treat.

Before you start your day

Think of one way you intend to pamper yourself today. Is there an art show you'd like to see, a movie you'd like to rent, or a second-hand shop you've been meaning to visit? Write down what you are going to do, with a time and how you'll get there, such as 'Today, I will walk to the National Portrait Gallery at 1pm to see the photography exhibition.' If you look on the treat as an appointment you'll be less likely to cancel it.

Getting ready

Don't just reach for your trusty old shirt and trousers. Choose a colour that reflects the way you'd like to feel today. Colours such as blue, green, white or red will not only make you look better than your usual black shirt, but you may feel better about yourself as well. So dig out that shirt you haven't worn for ages, or add an unusual pair of earrings or your favourite antique handbag. It's the little touches that count, not just to your overall appearance, but to the way you feel about yourself.

On your way to work

Treat yourself to a cup of your favourite imported coffee. Just one cup a day can lift your mood and increase your concentration levels.

Lunch

Remember, it's time to keep your appointment at the art gallery! Don't forget to drink your water. If your company doesn't have a water filter, splash out on a personal filter jug. Fill up your water bottle and remember to keep sipping.

Home time

If you don't feel like seeing a friend, going to the gym or going out, then go on an adventure. Try a different route home, going via an area you've always wanted to live in, or pass by a deli and pick up some delicious cheese or olives.

60-second mood-lifter

Place cotton wool balls between your toes. Now walk around the room for one full minute, taking care not to let any of the cotton balls fall out. It may seem silly, but when you're moody and irritable, it's because your energy is concentrated in the upper half of your body. This exercise will draw your focus to your feet and the ground, thus reconnecting your mind and body.

Day three

Morning glory

Now you're in the habit of waking up at the same time, make it a treat. Programme your stereo or radio to wake you with some soothing music, instead of a disembodied voice reading the news. It'll be less startling, and your body and mind will be stimulated by the tunes.

Breakfast

Whip up a delicious smoothie. Blend one banana, one egg, 150ml/5fl oz semi-skimmed milk and shavings of nutmeg. Blend until smooth. This is a great low-GI drink and will keep you full till lunchtime. Nutmeg is also thought to help boost your spirits.

Mid-morning

If you've been stuck at your desk all morning, take a break. Offer to get coffees for your office, or just go for a brisk walk to the newsagent's and buy the morning paper. Your eyes and mind will thank you!

60-second mood lifter

Buy yourself some flowers for your desk. Red tulips will help increase motivation, plus you'll smile every time you glance at them.

Lunch

Choose a low- to medium-GI snack, such as pea and ham soup, or a chicken salad.

Mid-afternoon

Check your liquid intake. Have you drunk two litres today? If not, top up!

After work

You had yesterday afternoon off, so it's exercise time. If you've had a hard day at work or looking after the family, choose a fitness class that gets your blood pumping. Try kickboxing or a weights class. This will force your mind to focus on something other than your stress levels.

Dinner

Have you had enough fish this week? Try a prawn salad, with lots of healthy additions, such as tomatoe, avocado, pine nuts, feta cheese and a lemon vinaigrette.

Time for bed

If you've been to the gym, relax your muscles with a warm bath. Light some candles, play some soothing music and add 250g/9oz of Epsom salts to the bath. It'll help heal sore, stiff muscles, so you won't suffer from any stiffness the next day.

Time for thanks

Before you go to sleep why not acknowledge your appreciation of the day? Write down everything you're grateful for, such as 'a sunny day', 'happy kids', or even something you achieved that day, such as going to the gym or keeping your temper when everything went wrong that morning. Sometimes it's easy to forget about all the positive things that happen; it's much easier to focus on what went wrong.

Day four

Morning glory

Start the day right with a hearty breakfast of scrambled eggs on rye bread. Yum! Add some smoked salmon for a special treat.

Exercise task

If it's a sunny day, why not go to work on foot or go for a brisk walk around the block? The dirty dishes will be there when you get back and that pile of work on your desk can wait. You'll be more likely to get through your busy day if you've taken time out for your mind and body.

Lunch

Take yourself out to lunch. Even if it's just the corner café, granting yourself an hour to leisurely eat your lunch and read the paper or your favourite magazine is a lovely way to break up the day and give yourself some 'me' time.

Mid-afternoon

Tempted to reach for that chocolate bar? We know it's much nicer than fruit, so let's compromise. Enjoy a dark-chocolate bar, organic if possible. Nutritionists now say that a small amount of dark chocolate each day can help lower blood pressure, reduce PMT and raise your mood.

After work

If you don't go out to work, then you may find that your day is centred around your children and their needs. Try to combine your needs with theirs: take the kids to the park and play frisbee. It'll improve their co-ordination and exercise levels, and it's a great family bonding experience.

Dinner

Take the night off. Ask your partner to cook or order a takeaway. But don't be tempted to overindulge. Stick to vegetable-based sauces, and avoid anything with cream. You'll just feel overfed and exhausted afterwards.

Time for bed

If you're used to leaving the cleaning and washing until the weekend, now's your chance to get a head-start on your chores. Spend no more than 1½ hours putting things right: clean the kitchen and bathroom, and sort out your laundry. When the weekend comes you'll appreciate having crossed off some of your tasks already.

60-second mood-lifter

Drink up. No, not just water, but another good tipple. Researchers now say that two glasses of red wine a day helps to lower blood pressure and avoid heart disease. Stick to two glasses only!

Day five

Morning glory

If you started this plan on Monday, then day five means only one thing… it's Friday! Don't let all your hard work go downhill. When you get up and while you're waiting for the kettle to boil or the water to heat up, use the time to do some exercise. Stand with your feet shoulder-width apart, tighten your buttocks, and bend your knees, slowly lowering your upper body vertically downwards into the squat position. Hold for three breaths and then return to normal. Repeat at least 20 times.

Breakfast

It's Friday so spoil yourself. Add some smoked salmon to your scrambled eggs, for an omega-3-rich meal. Garnish with cracked pepper and place on rye bread for a truly decadent meal.

Mid-morning

Don't leave all your chores for the weekend. Spend 20 minutes making sure that your bills have been paid or that you have food for the weekend. Don't traipse to the store, use your time wisely and order your groceries online and have them delivered Saturday morning (not too early!). Many home delivery companies offer free delivery if your order is above a certain amount.

Lunch

Don't let your good work slip. If everyone else is heading to the pub, join them, but avoid indulging in an alcoholic tipple. Instead, try a lime and soda, or a lemonade, lime and angostura bitters mix – it's sweet and refreshing, and you'll still be able to concentrate all afternoon.

Mid-afternoon

Our brains tend to slow down in the afternoon, which means we're less likely to be creative or motivated to complete difficult tasks. There's no point fighting nature, so use the dead time in the afternoon to sort out your filing, sign off any outstanding paperwork or answer any emails that have been lingering in your in-box. Leaving work with a clear mind and desk on Friday afternoon means that you'll start Monday morning with a spring in your step.

After work

To gym or not to gym? That is the million-dollar question on a Friday night! Of course it's tempting to follow everyone else down to the pub for a few drinks, but you could end up staggering home, stopping off to grab a fatty takeaway and falling into your bed.

There is a happy compromise. If you go to the work gym, or one nearby, go for just 30 minutes. You'll release the stresses and fulfil your exercise requirements for the day. Then go and meet your friends for a drink. You'll be less likely to overdo it, as you'll feel virtuous from your workout. Or, you may want to do something else entirely, such as seeing a movie or a show or even go out for dinner. All you have to do is change the focus of your evening to you and your health and happiness.

Dinner

Friday night is a tempting time to eat leftovers or a fatty takeaway. If your not eating out why not start the weekend with some (healthy) indulgences. Stop by the deli and buy some Swiss cheese, freshly made hummus and rye bread or wheat-free crackers. Accompanied by a bottle of red wine, this carpet picnic is an ideal way to wind down after your long, hard week and gives you (and your partner, if you have one) a chance to catch up on your lives.

Time for bed

Friday night can be stressful if you've had a busy week. The thought of all that work waiting for you, the amount of money you've spent, the amount of money that hasn't arrived as promised... all these things tend to crowd our brains on Friday night, when we should be winding down. Remember, there is nothing you can do about work-related problems on a Friday night. What you can do is write down what is worrying you and, if possible or relevant, write down a possible solution next to it. Even if the solution is 'wait until Tuesday when we have our monthly meeting', it means that you have prioritised your problems and allocated them a time to be solved or addressed.

Day six

Yippee! It's the weekend! Don't give into temptation to have a nice sleep-in. Sleeping in will only upset your body clock and make it even more difficult to wake up with the alarm on Monday morning. Waking up at the same time as you do during the week can be bliss. After all, waking up and knowing that you don't have to get out of bed is a wonderful feeling. Try to do the following:

- Get out of bed, get dressed and get the newspapers.
- Make yourself a cup of tea, a fresh juice and a piece of toast.
- Retire to the sofa, the garden or back to bed. Don't get back under the covers though.
- Spend a couple of hours reading the newspapers and having a leisurely cup of tea and breakfast. Many people find that they wake up at the weekend feeling slightly fuzzy-headed. This may be due to dehydration, particularly if you have been drinking about 2 litres of water per day or you have a regular morning coffee to start your day. Your body may be experiencing a slight detox, so try to follow your usual routine.

Mid-morning

It's tempting to get started on the housework, but wait! This is your weekend after all. Instead, go for a morning workout, yoga class, or 40-minute walk and then get started on the chores.

Lunch

You've exercised hard this morning – housework burns around 250 calories an hour – so you're probably hungry. Don't skip meals at the weekend; stick to your normal eating schedule. Since you've got some time, make an occasion of lunch. A fresh salad with grilled chicken is ideal. It's filling, but also nutritious.

Mid-afternoon

Don't be tempted to fill every hour with tasks. Spending an hour doing absolutely nothing may sound like bliss, but many people find it virtually impossible to turn off. Lie outside in the garden, or go to the park. Watch the clouds float by and let your troubles go with them.

Evening

Try not to overdo the alcohol and food at the weekend, even though you think you can use the next day to recover. Your Happy Plan is for every single day – there's no allowance for a hangover!

Bedtime

Try to go to bed at the same time as a weekday. Run a warm bath and spend at least 20 minutes just floating in the water. Light some tea lights, add some relaxing oil, such as lavender or chang may, and practise one of the meditation exercises in this book.

60-second mood-lifter

If you're feeling a little low, call a friend for a giggle and a gossip (or a rant and a moan!). Talking your problems through or just catching up with each other's lives, can help to shake you out of your world. And a good laugh does you, your health, and even your waistline the world of good!

Day seven

Morning!

As your body is now in a routine, so you'll probably find that 10 minutes or so after waking up you'll want to get moving. Boost your serotonin levels with some morning sex – either with your partner or solo! – which will raise your heart beat and release feel-good pheromones.

Breakfast

There's nothing tastier than a fry-up and it doesn't have to be unhealthy. Swap the white bread for rye bread, grill the bacon and forego the sausages. Add some antioxidants through grilled tomatoes, and mushrooms, which have lots of vitamin B. Poach, grill or scramble your eggs, but be strict with the amount of butter you use. Serve with a big mug of tea, coffee or your favourite herbal brew.

Mid-morning

Spend some time doing the crossword. It doesn't have to be the super-dooper cryptic version, the easy one is just as good. Challenging your brain in some way is a good method of keeping your memory cells motivated and may even help ward off Alzheimer's disease.

Lunch

You may be full from breakfast, so a light lunch of smoked salmon with cream cheese on a bagel may be sufficient.

Mid-afternoon

There's nothing better than a Sunday afternoon nap either in bed or on your sofa or in the garden. Set the alarm clock for 40 minutes and, as long as it's before 3pm (any later can interfere with your sleep cycle and prevent you getting to sleep at night), then snooze away!

Even if you don't have a garden, plan to spend some time on the weekend amongst nature – walking in the country or a nearby park.

60-second mood lifter

Researchers say that gardening is a great way to help lift your mood and help you burn calories. Digging your fingers into the earth and feeling the moistness and goodness can help you to refocus your mind. If you don't have your own garden, enquire about allotments or volunteering at a garden centre or your nearest park.

Evening

You've worked hard all week, so your reward will be a tasty Sunday meal. Either visit your local pub or restaurant for a real treat or spend a couple of hours cooking your own. There's no rush, so take your time. If you've got a stressful week ahead, try a roast chicken or turkey, as the tryptophan in these meats will help prepare and protect your body against the coming demands.

Don't spend Sunday night bemoaning the fact that the weekend is over. It's not! Go to a movie or visit some friends, or even go for a steam at the gym. Anything that gets you out of the habit of watching the clock and counting down the hours till it's time to go to bed.

When it is bedtime, take 10 minutes to get your clothes ready for the following day. Pack any dinner leftovers into a lunch container and make sure you have all the work paraphernalia you need: fully charged mobile phone, money, transport ticket, etc.

Index

Acknowledgements

I would like to thank the following organisations who selflessly gave their time and advice to help with the writing of this book:

British Acupuncture Council on 020 8735 0400 www.acupuncture.org.uk

The Mental Health Foundation
Sea Containers House
20 Upper Ground, London, SE1 9QB
Tel: 020 7803 1130

Efalex for information on Omega 3s
visit www.efamol.com
Tel: 0870 6060128.

I'd also like to thank several people for their support, guidance and encouragement while writing this book: Vicky Pemberton, Natalie Savona, Susan Elderkin and Alaina Wall: thank you for the supportive phone calls, bottles of wine and friendship. To my parents, Colleen and Bob and my sister Cherie. And to Conn, who constantly reminds me what true happiness is.

Picture credits